I0824297

NEUTRAL GROUND

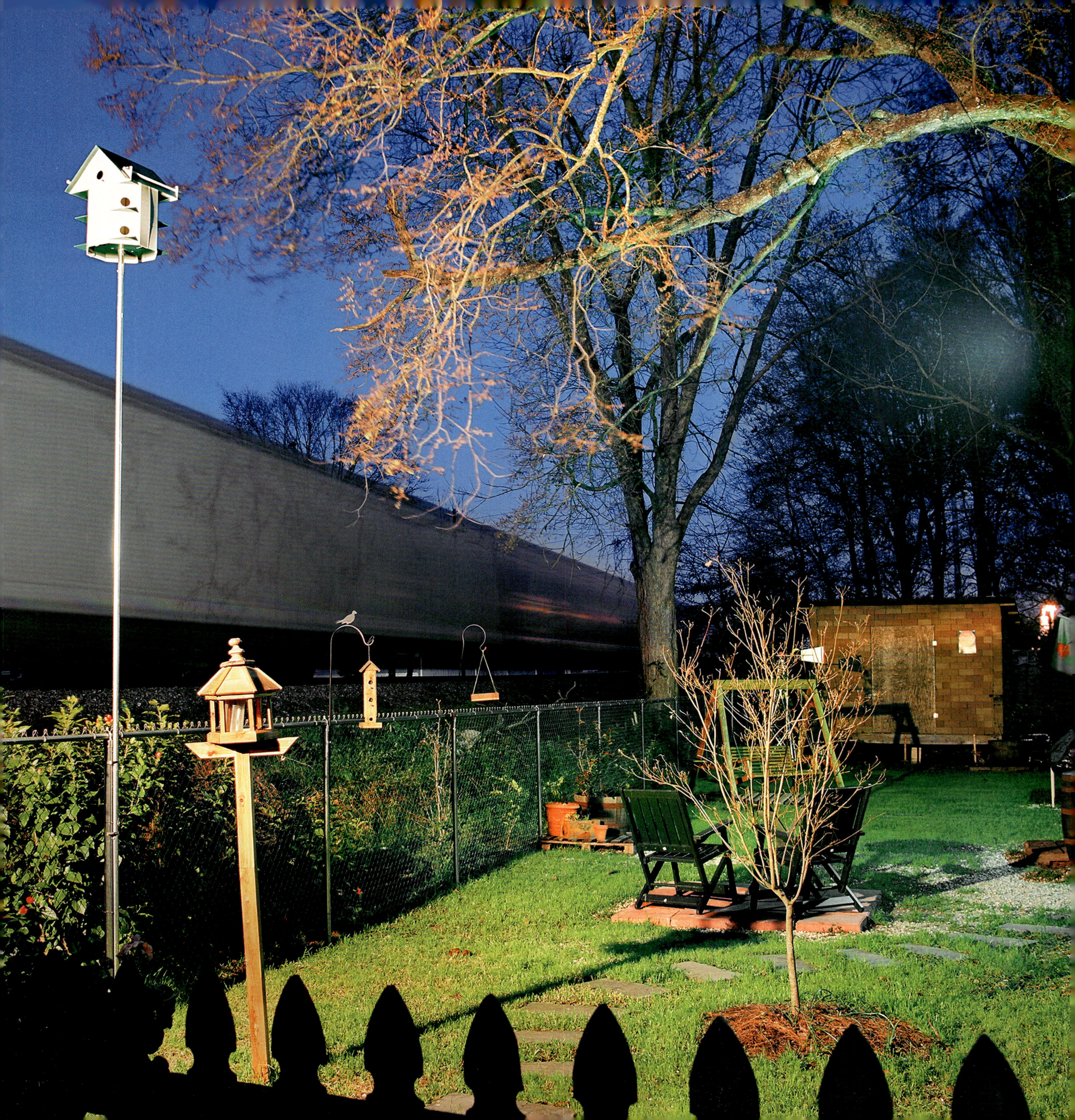

NEUTRAL GROUND

NEW ORLEANS 1990–2005

WILLIAM GREINER

UNIVERSITY OF NEW ORLEANS PRESS | 2025

NEUTRAL GROUND: New Orleans 1990-2005

ISBN: 9781608014026

Cover and book design by Bonnie Campbell

University of New Orleans Press
FIRST EDITION

Printed in Italy on acid-free paper

UNIVERSITY OF NEW ORLEANS PRESS
2000 Lakeshore Drive
New Orleans, Louisiana 70148
unopress.org

CONTENTS

Foreword 1

Photographs 2–85

Artist Statement 87

Acknowledgments 89

FOREWORD

In New Orleans what other cities called a median, the raised strip of land separating lanes of traffic, is called the neutral ground. It plays a prominent role in the history, culture, and life of New Orleans. Millions of residents and visitors to the city use the neutral ground every year to jog, walk dogs past monuments erected there, watch parades, and board and step from streetcars. Neutral ground originally defined the area in the middle of Canal Street that separated Creole and Anglo neighborhoods. The neutral ground on Saint Charles Avenue contains streetcar tracks as well as a place for crowds to gather to watch Mardi Gras parades close up. It also means a place where one is safe from traffic. The word neutral means an impartial or unbiased place.

The title of this book, *Neutral Ground*, becomes a metaphor for where William Greiner stands as a photographer. He shoots from the point of view of an observer, an artist without fear because he is shooting the world from the safety of his ground—his talent.

—JOHN RAMSEY MILLER

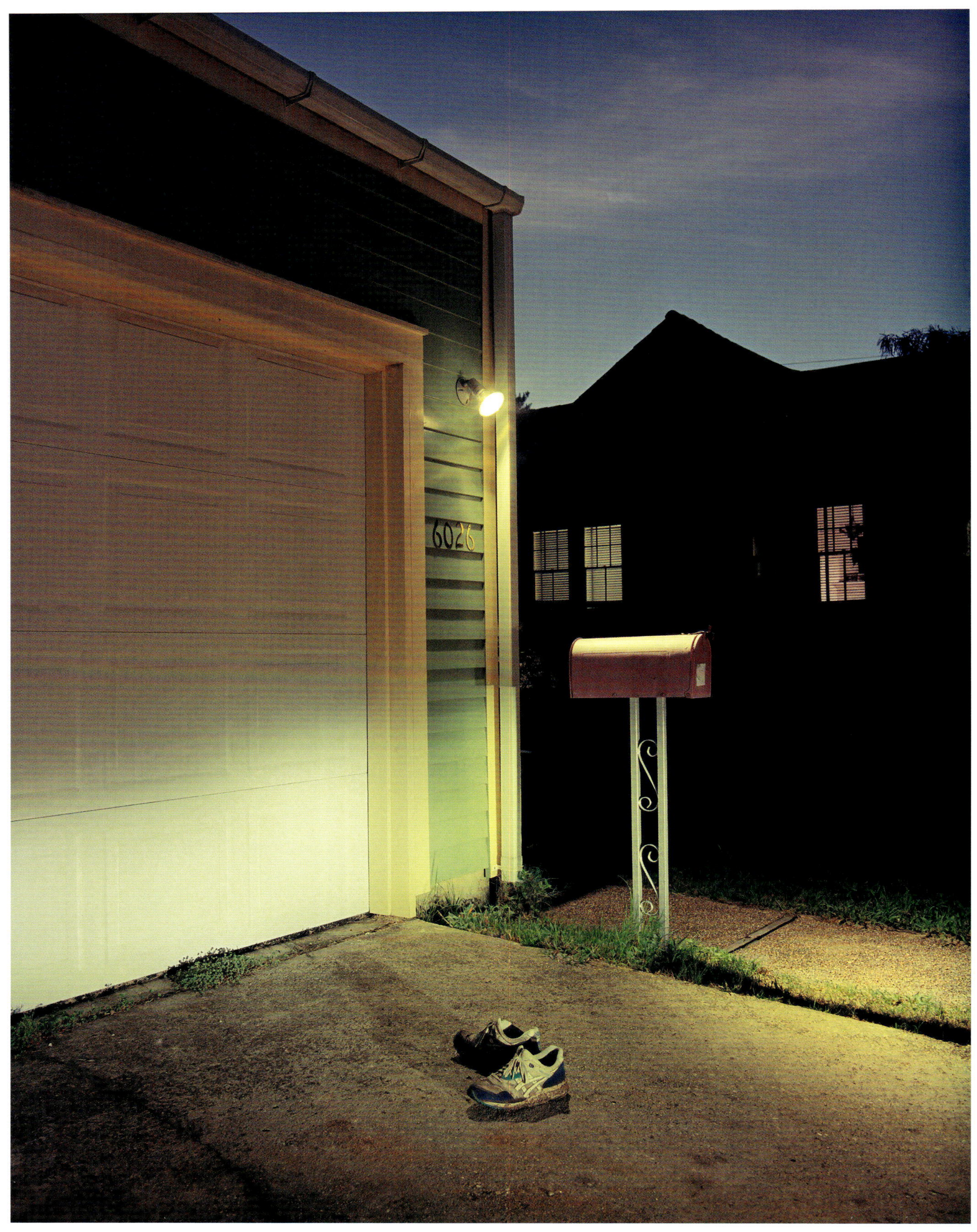
6026

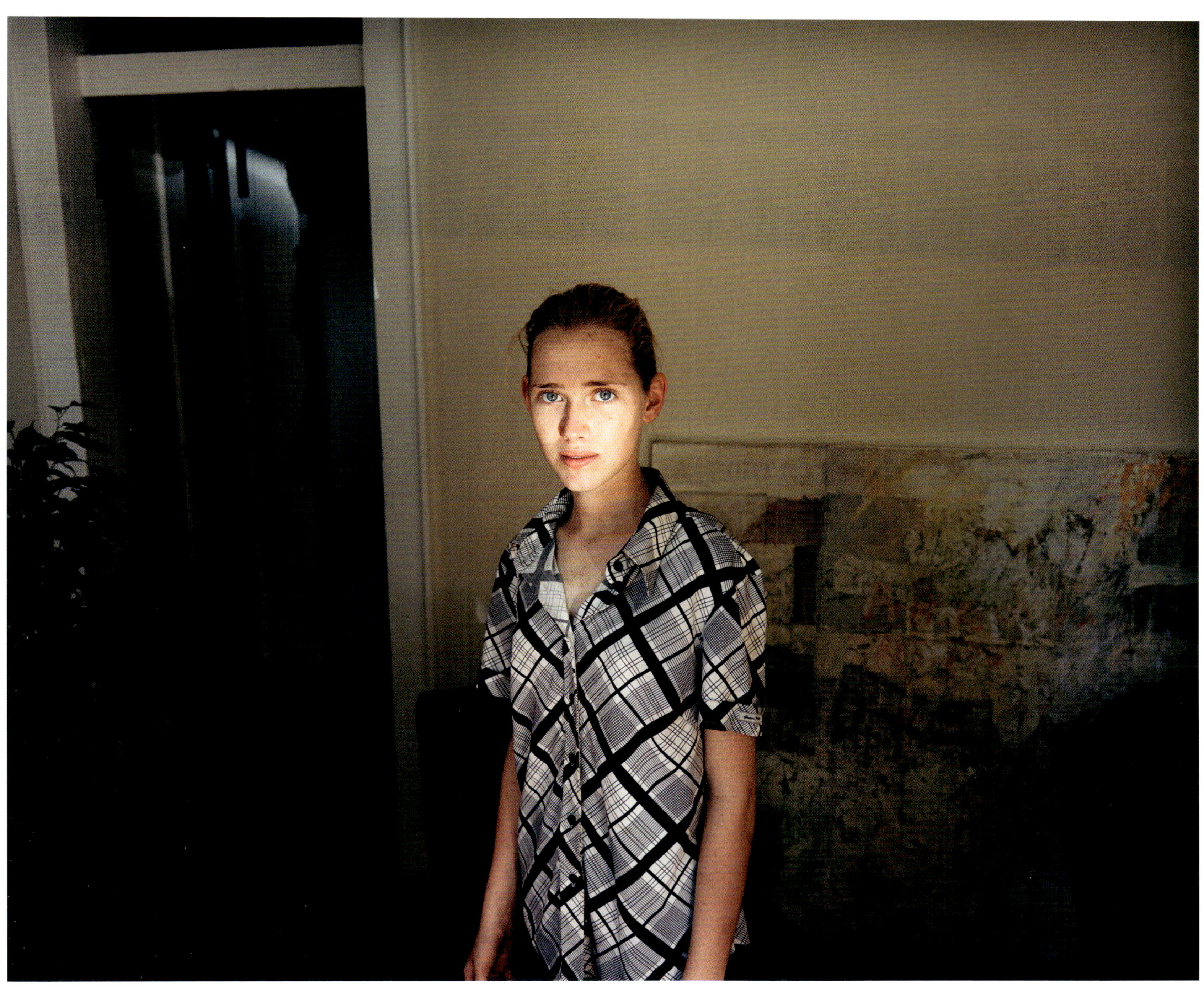

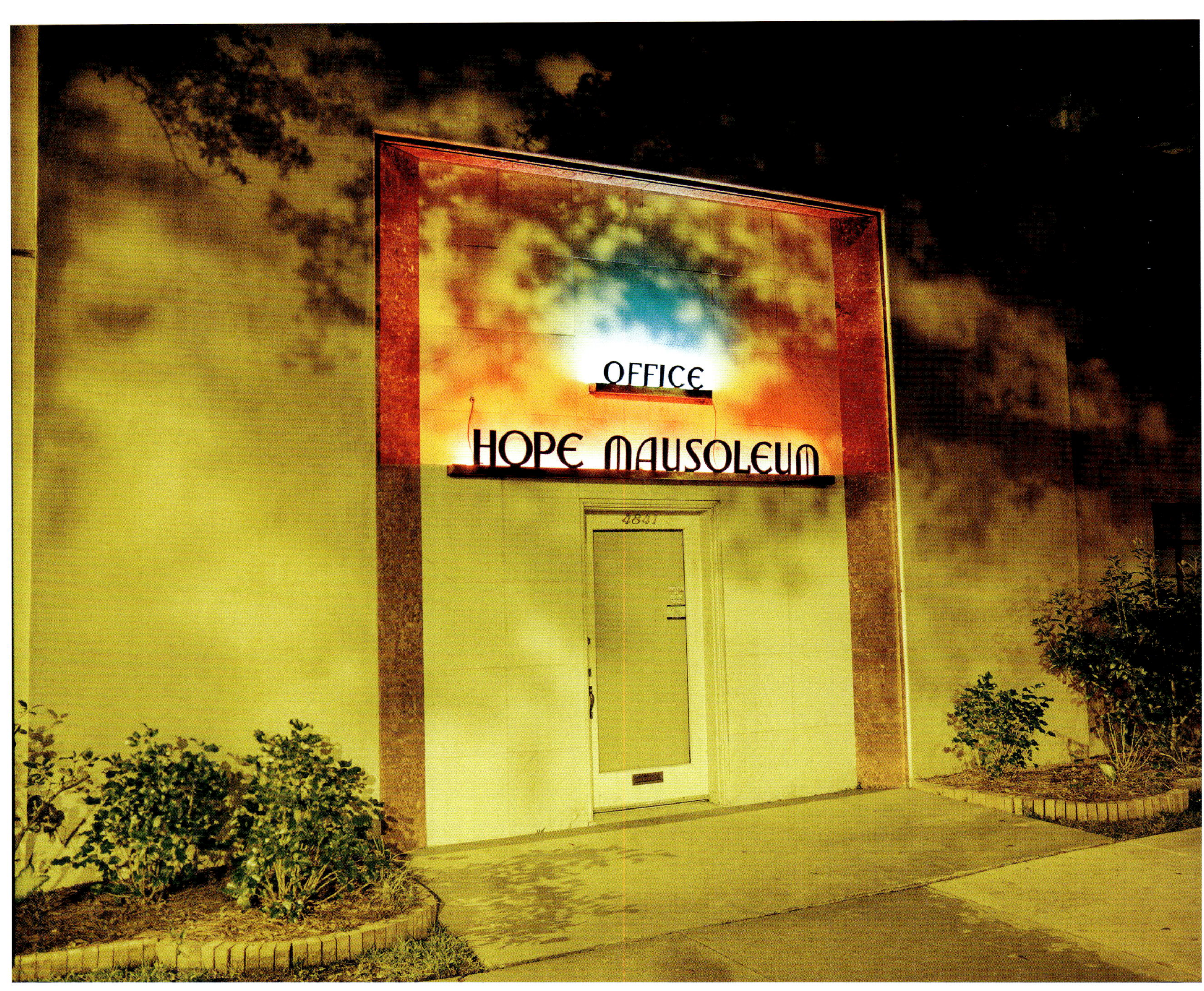
OFFICE
HOPE MAUSOLEUM
4841

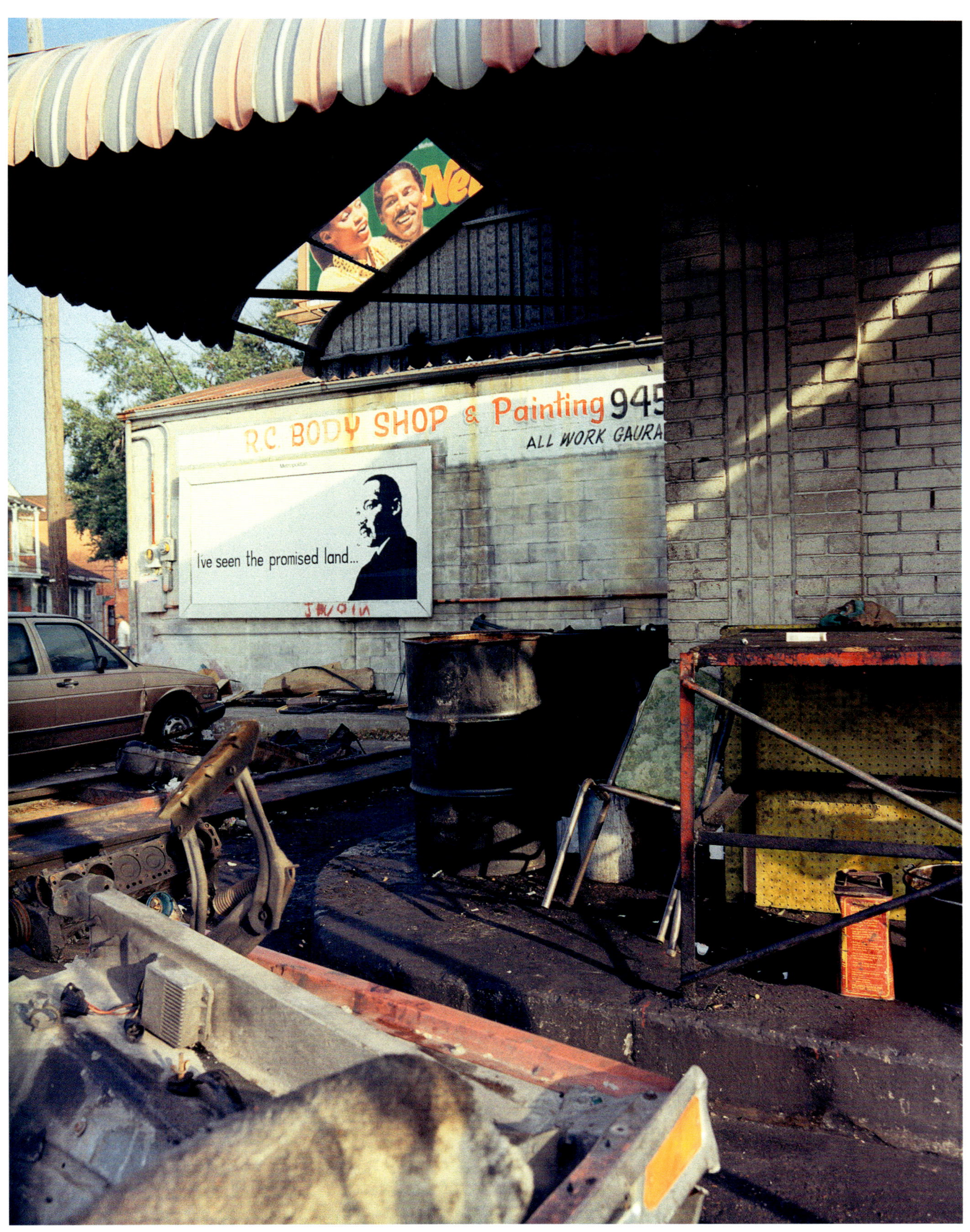
R.C. BODY SHOP & Painting 945
ALL WORK GAURA
I've seen the promised land...

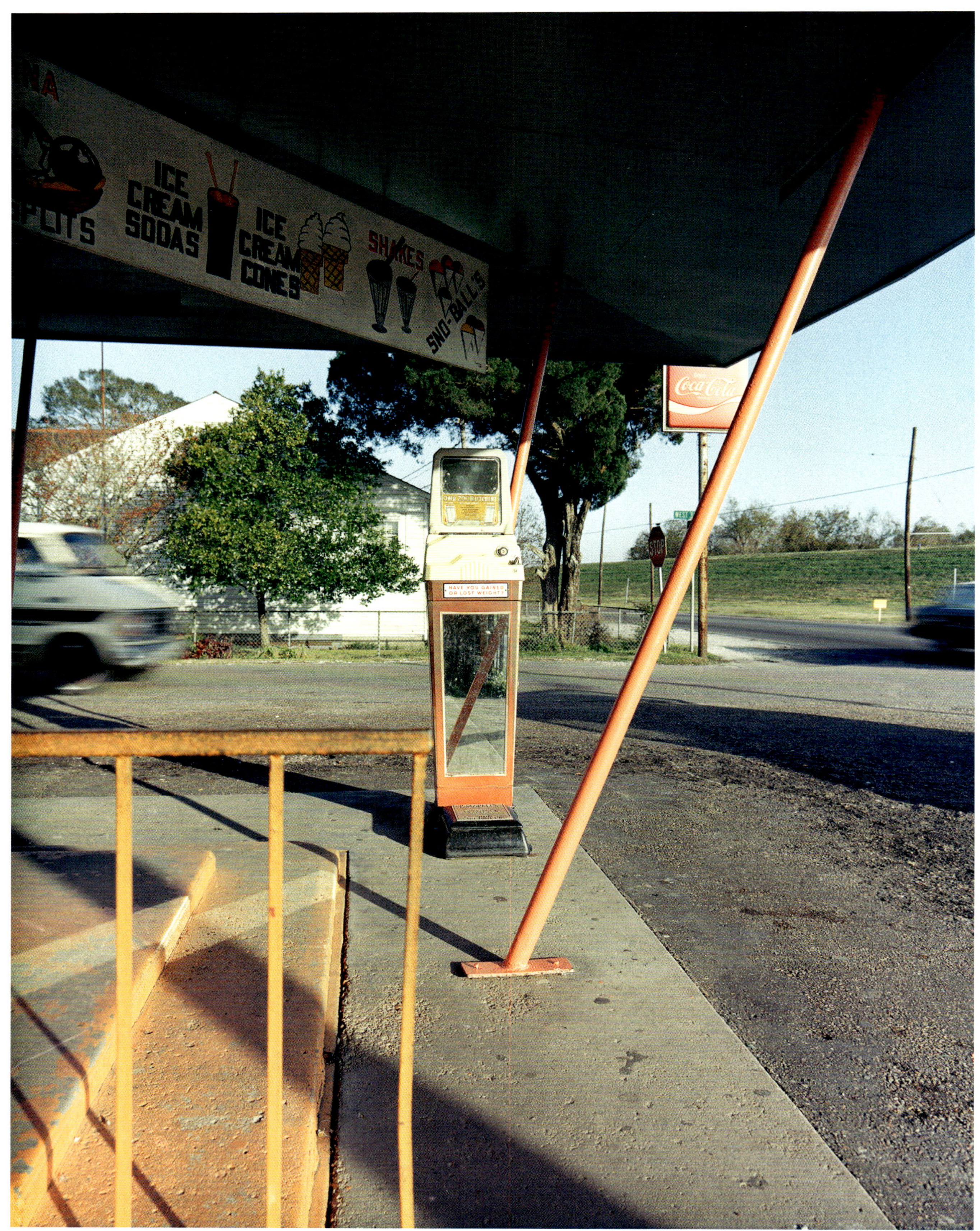
ICE CREAM SODAS
ICE CREAM CONES
SHAKES
SNO-BALL'S
Coca-Cola
STOP
HAVE YOU GAINED OR LOST WEIGHT?

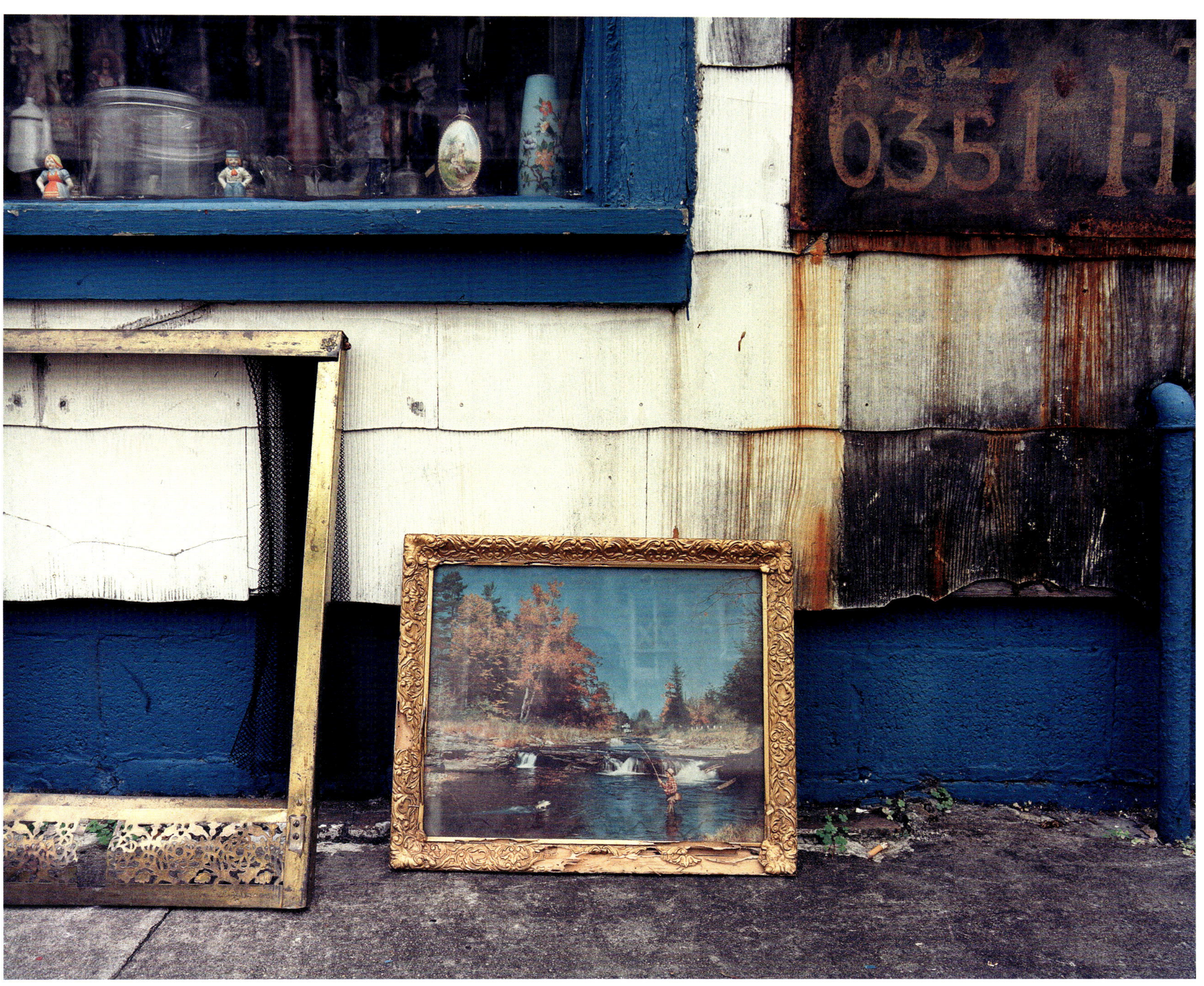
JA 2
6351

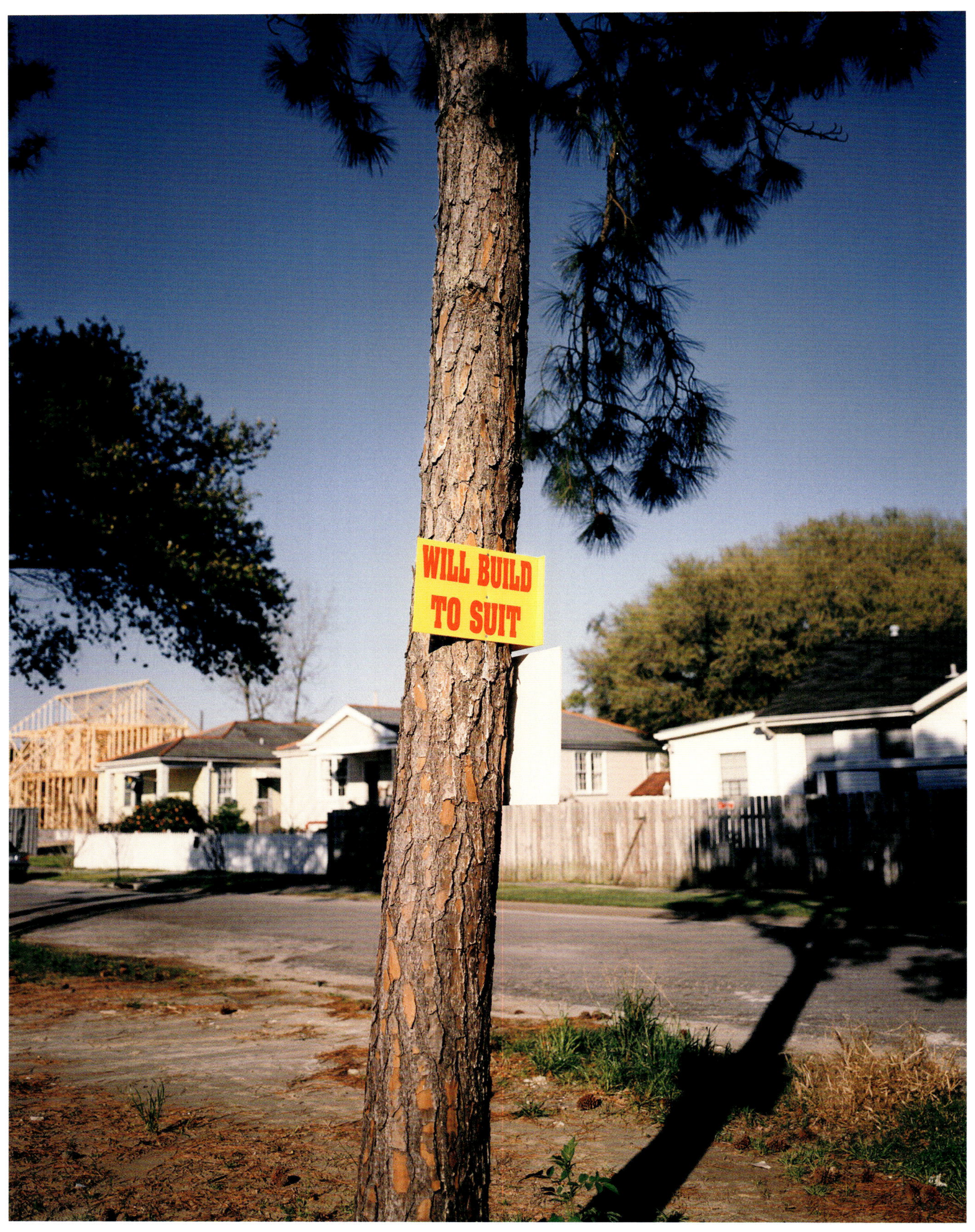
WILL BUILD
TO SUIT

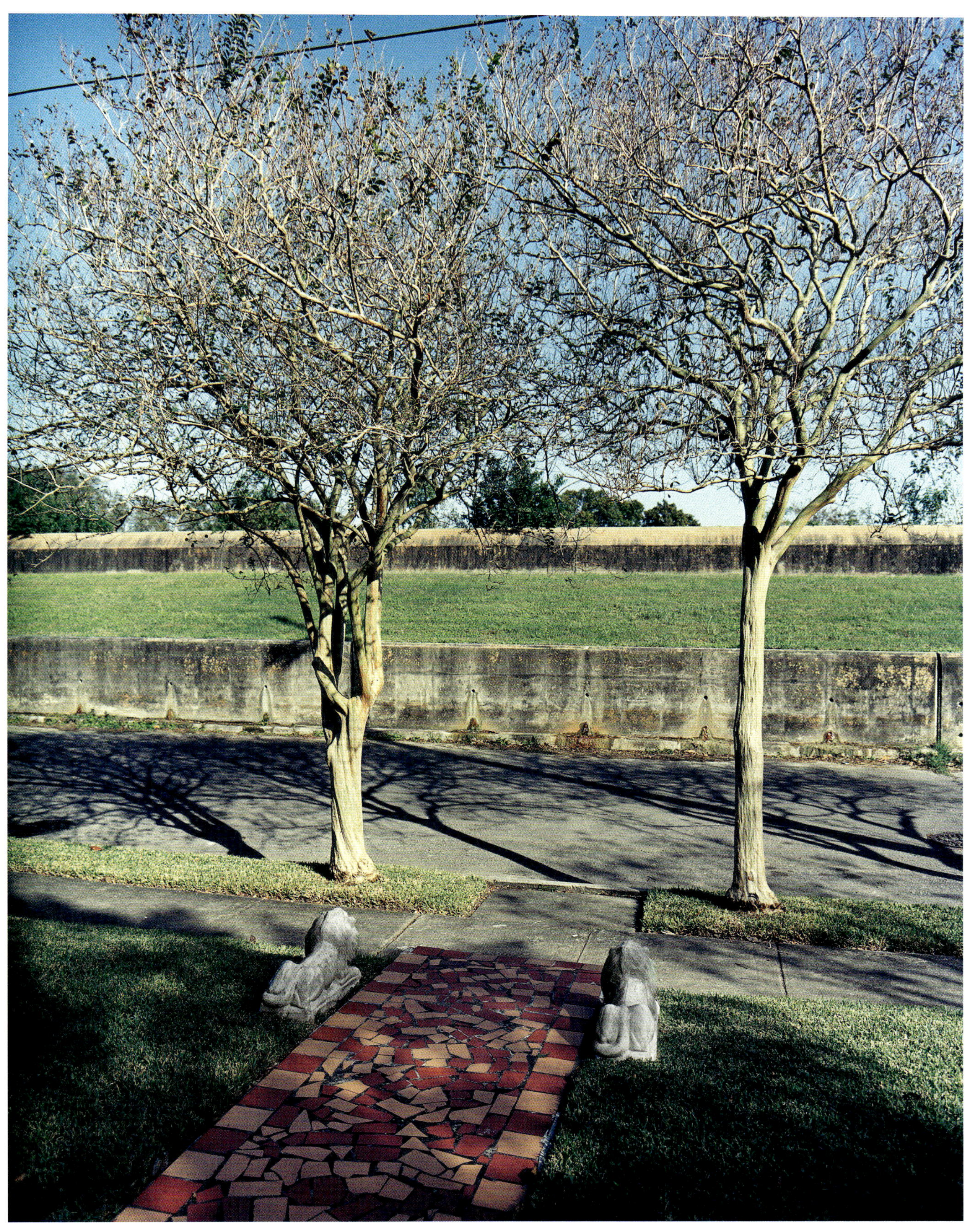

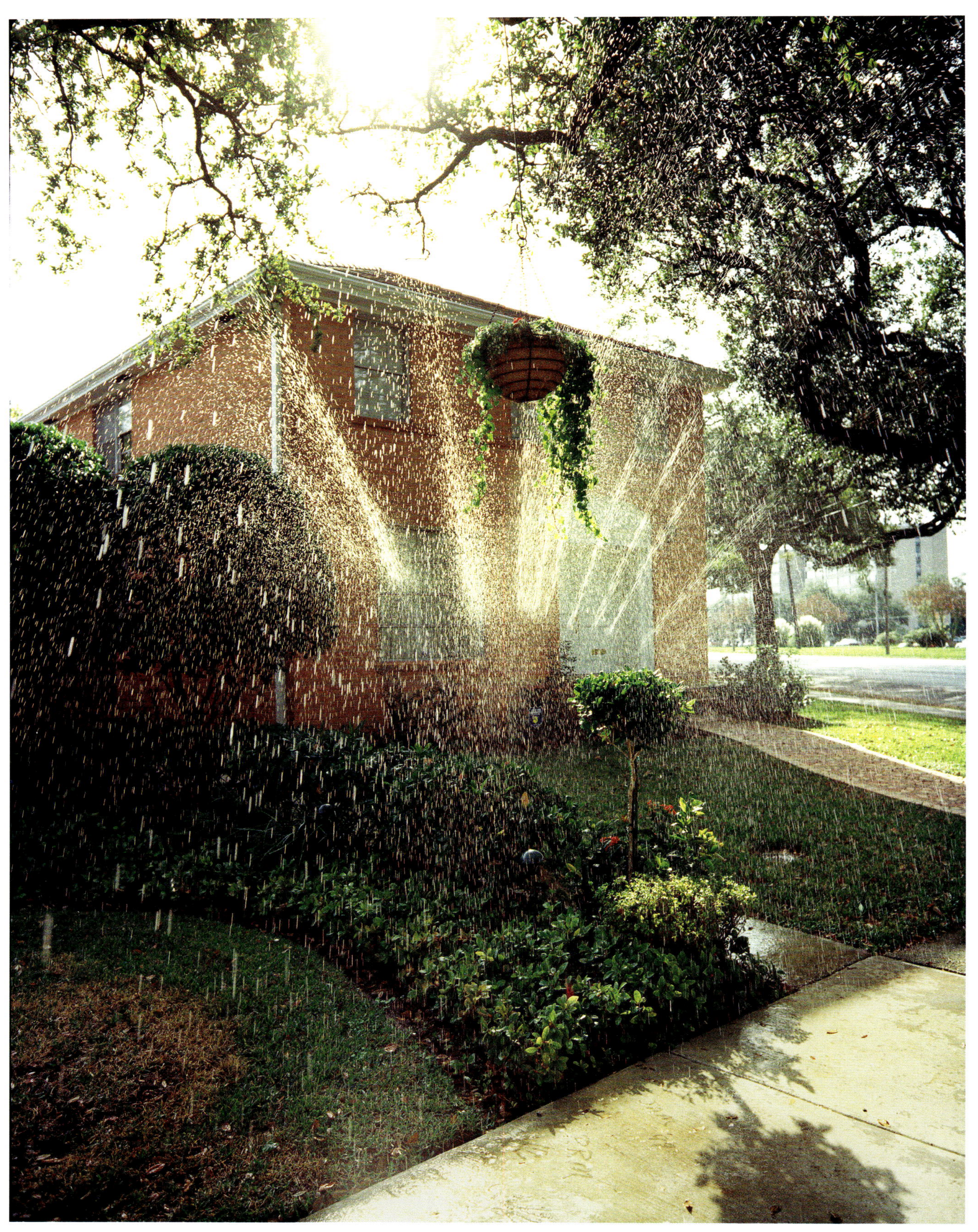

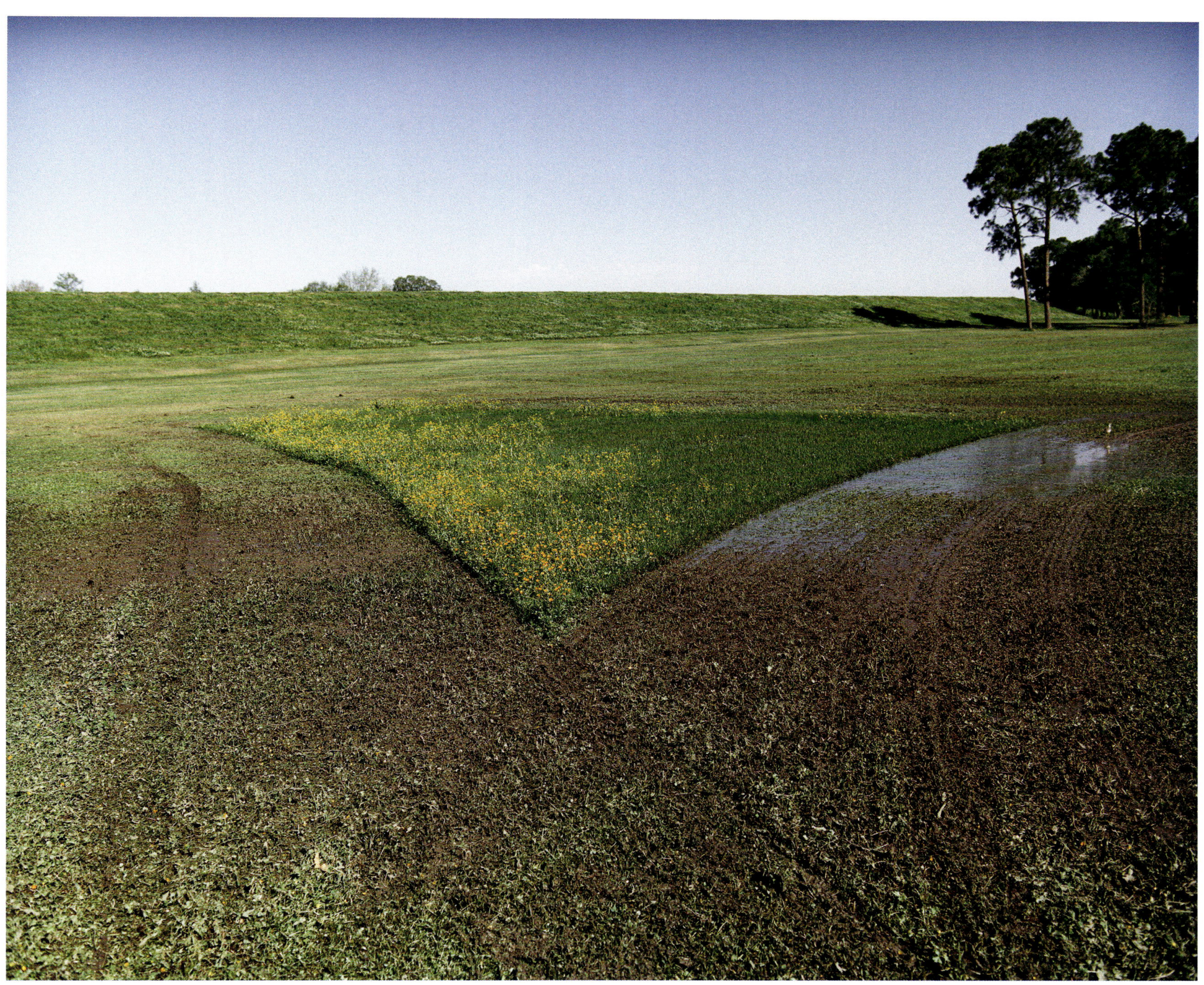

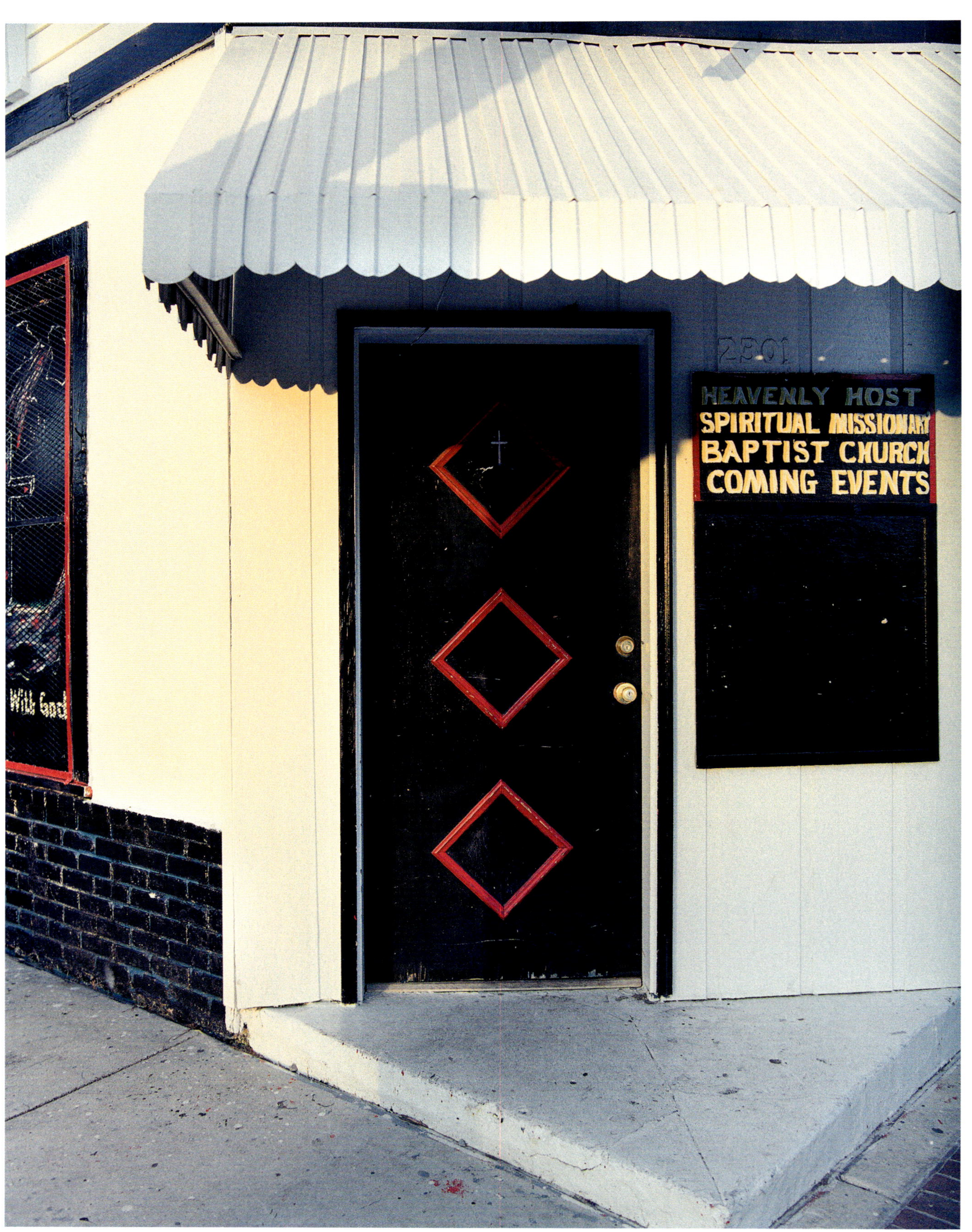
HEAVENLY HOST
SPIRITUAL MISSIONARY
BAPTIST CHURCH
COMING EVENTS
With God

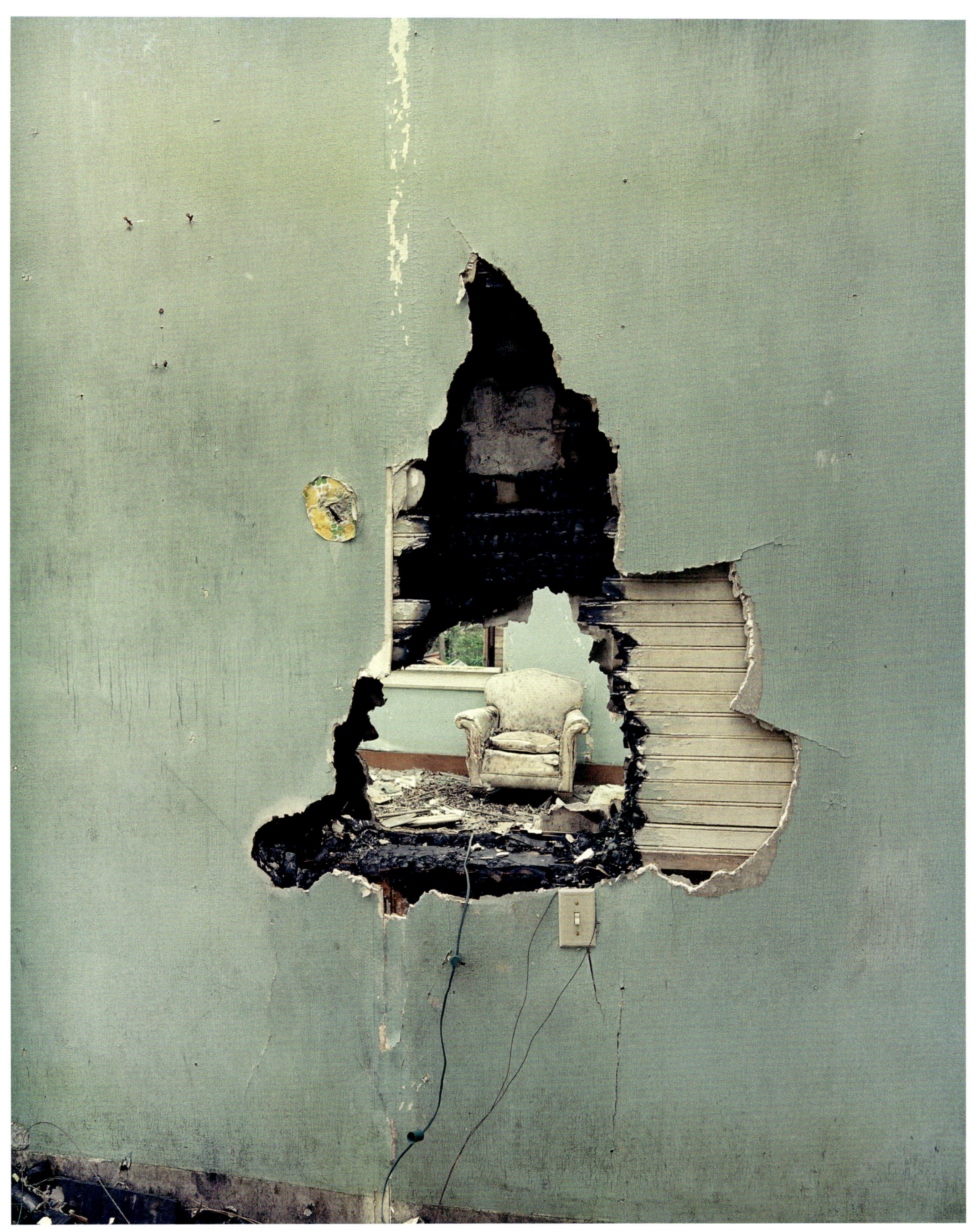

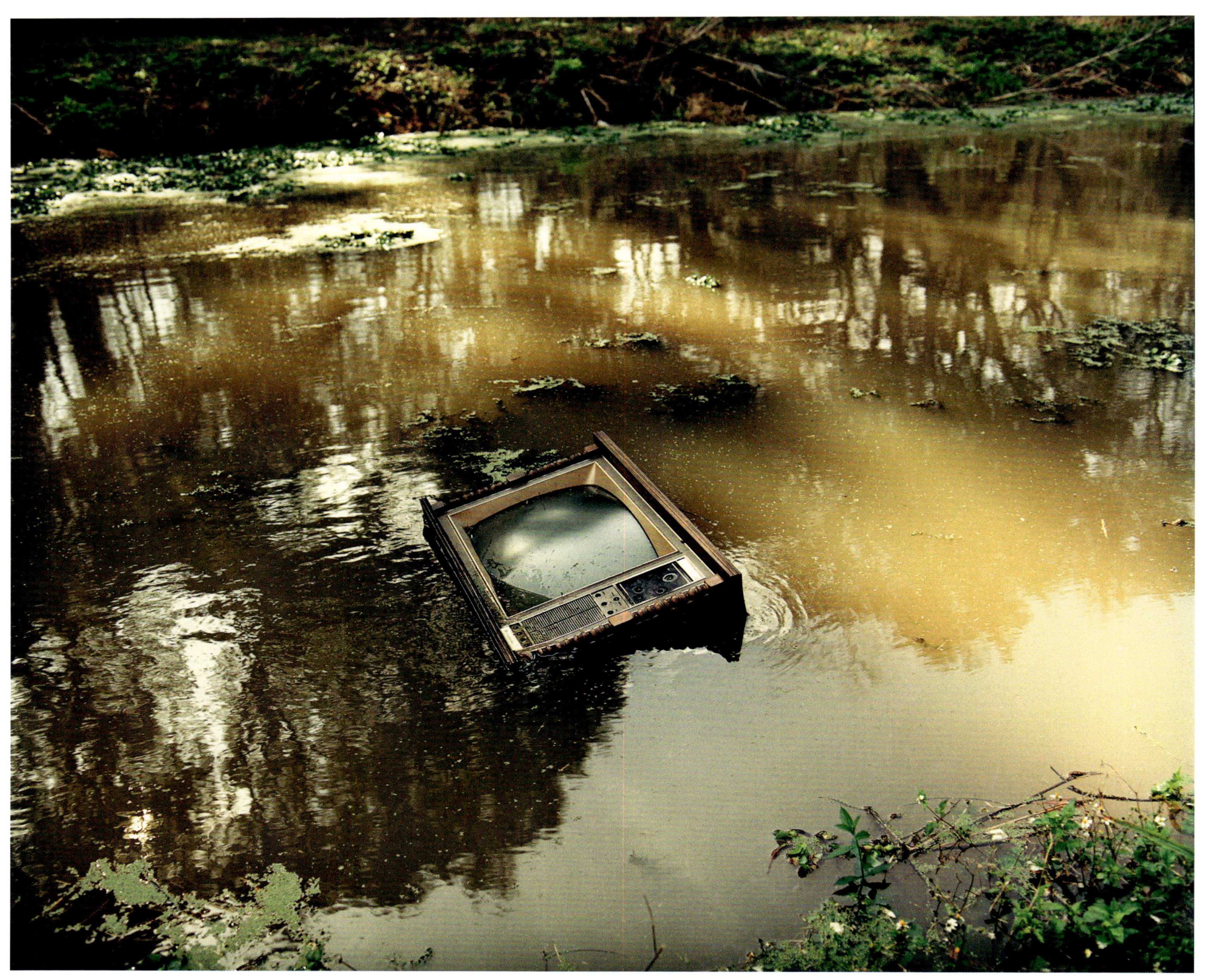

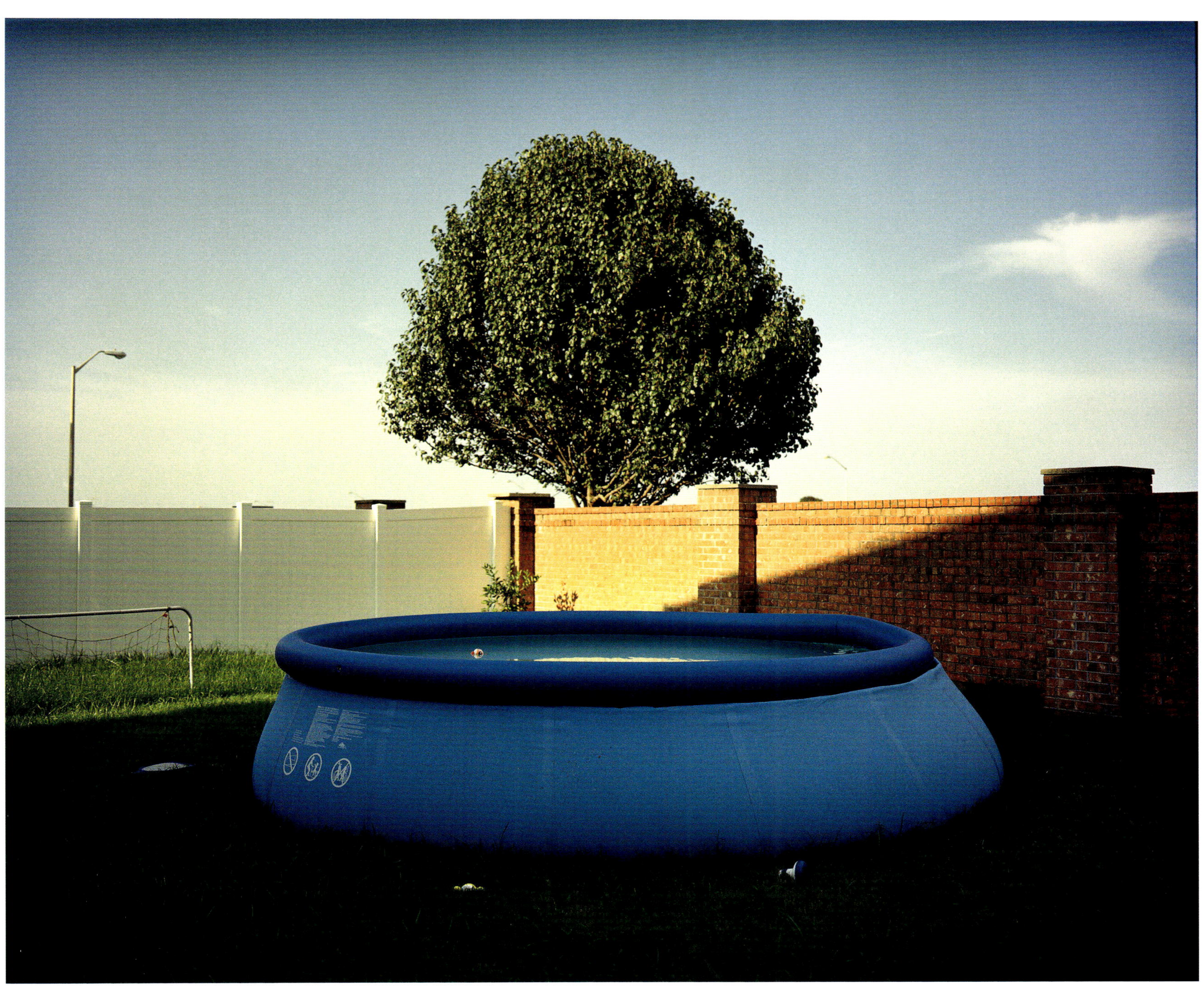

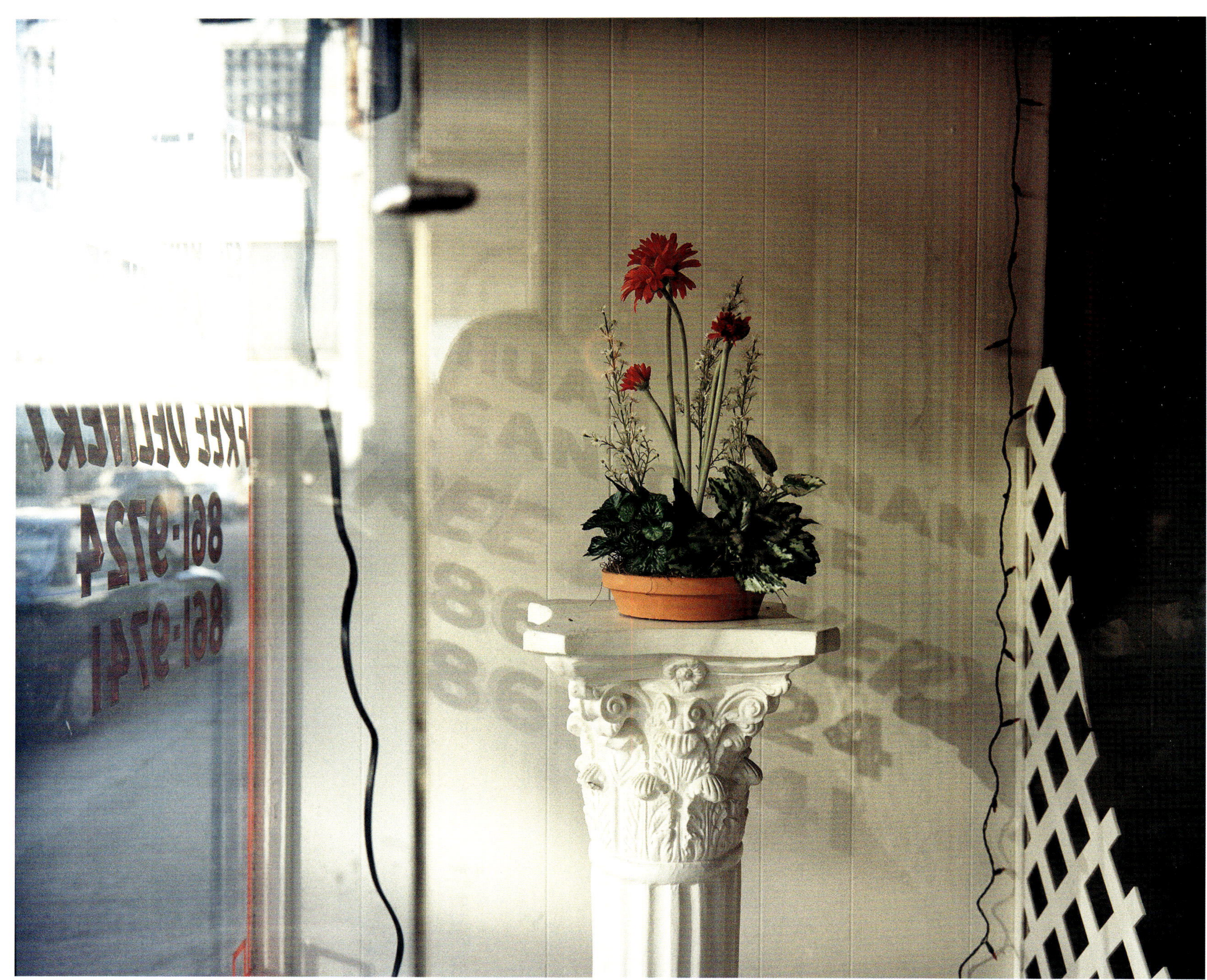
861-9724
861-9741

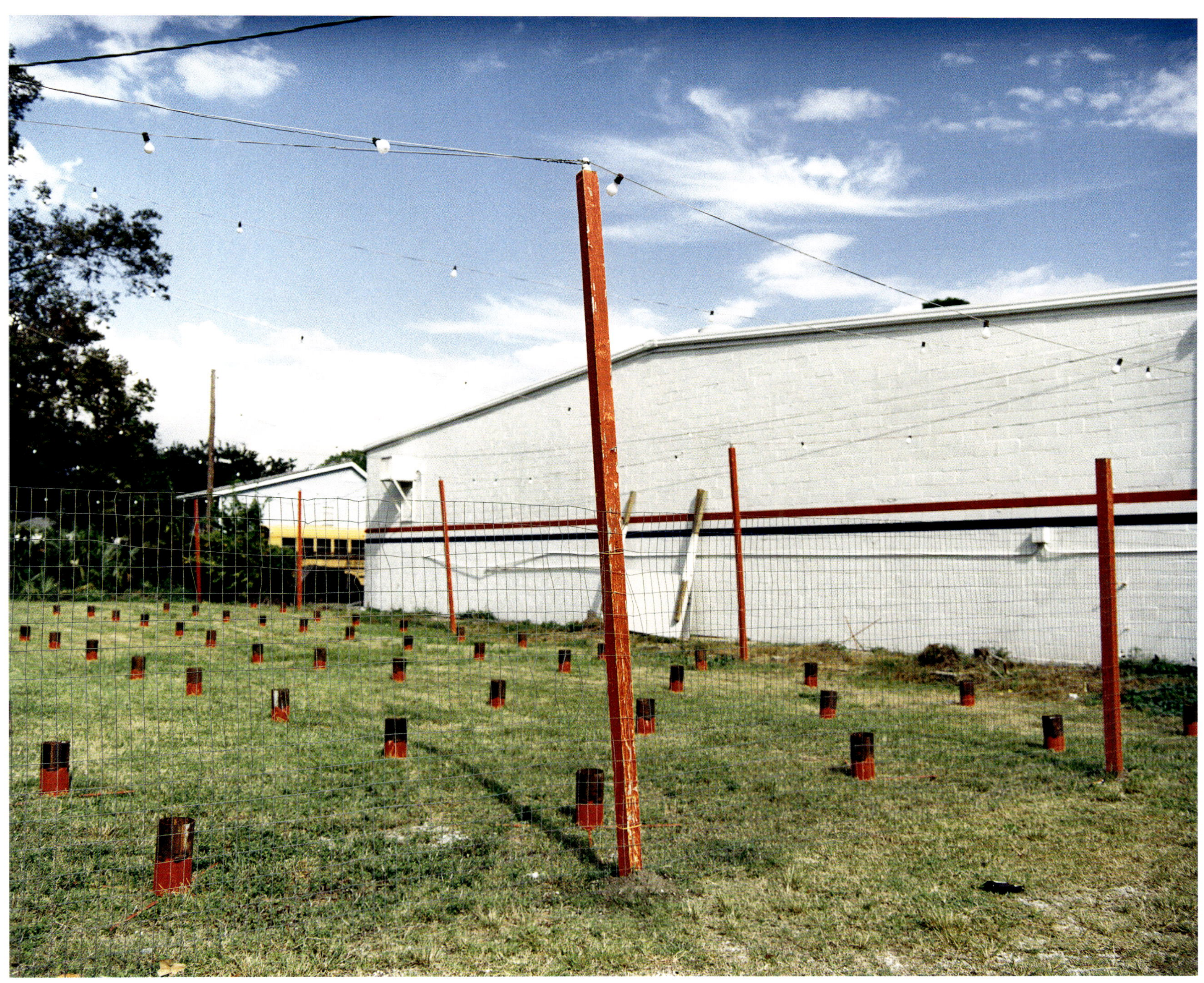

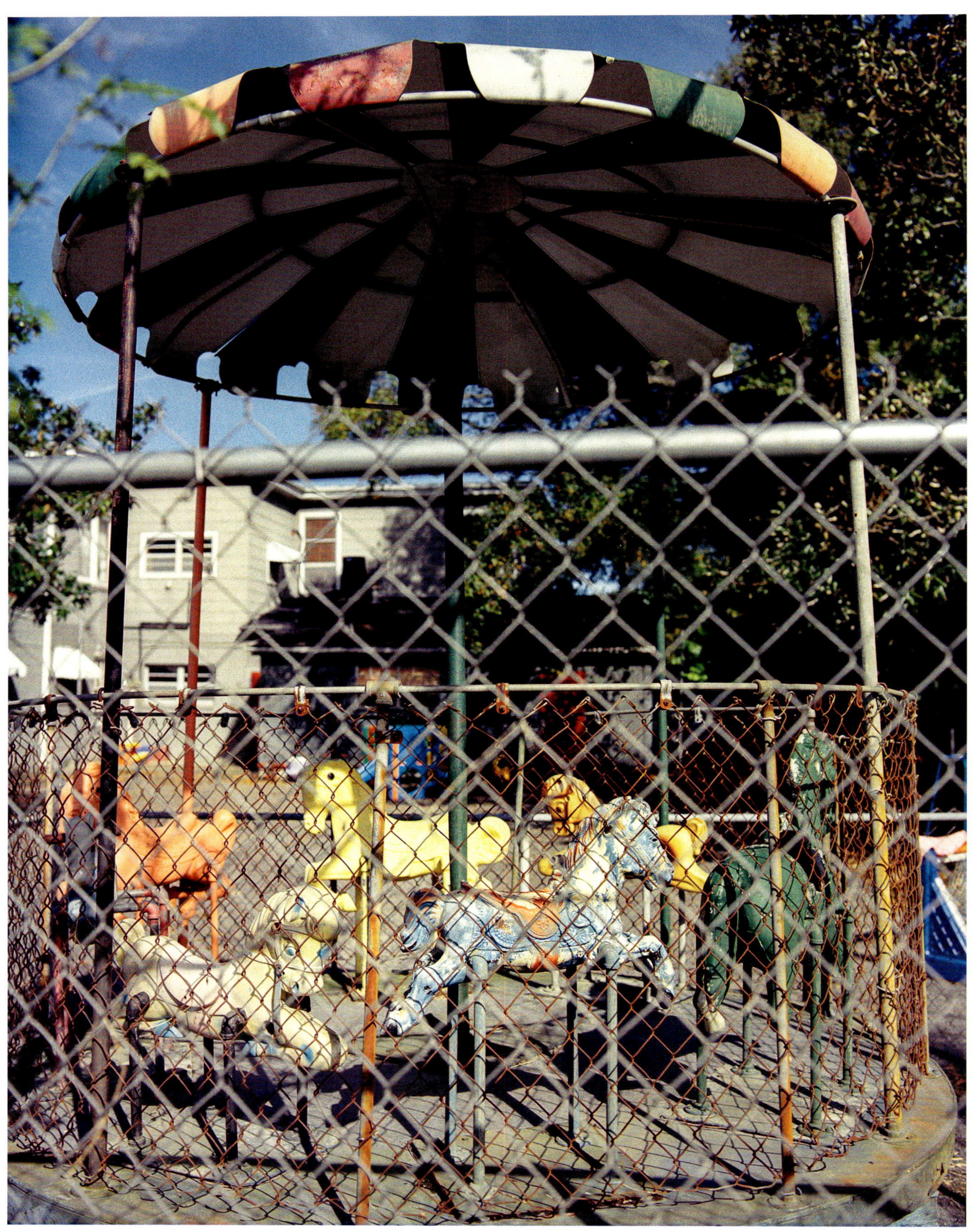

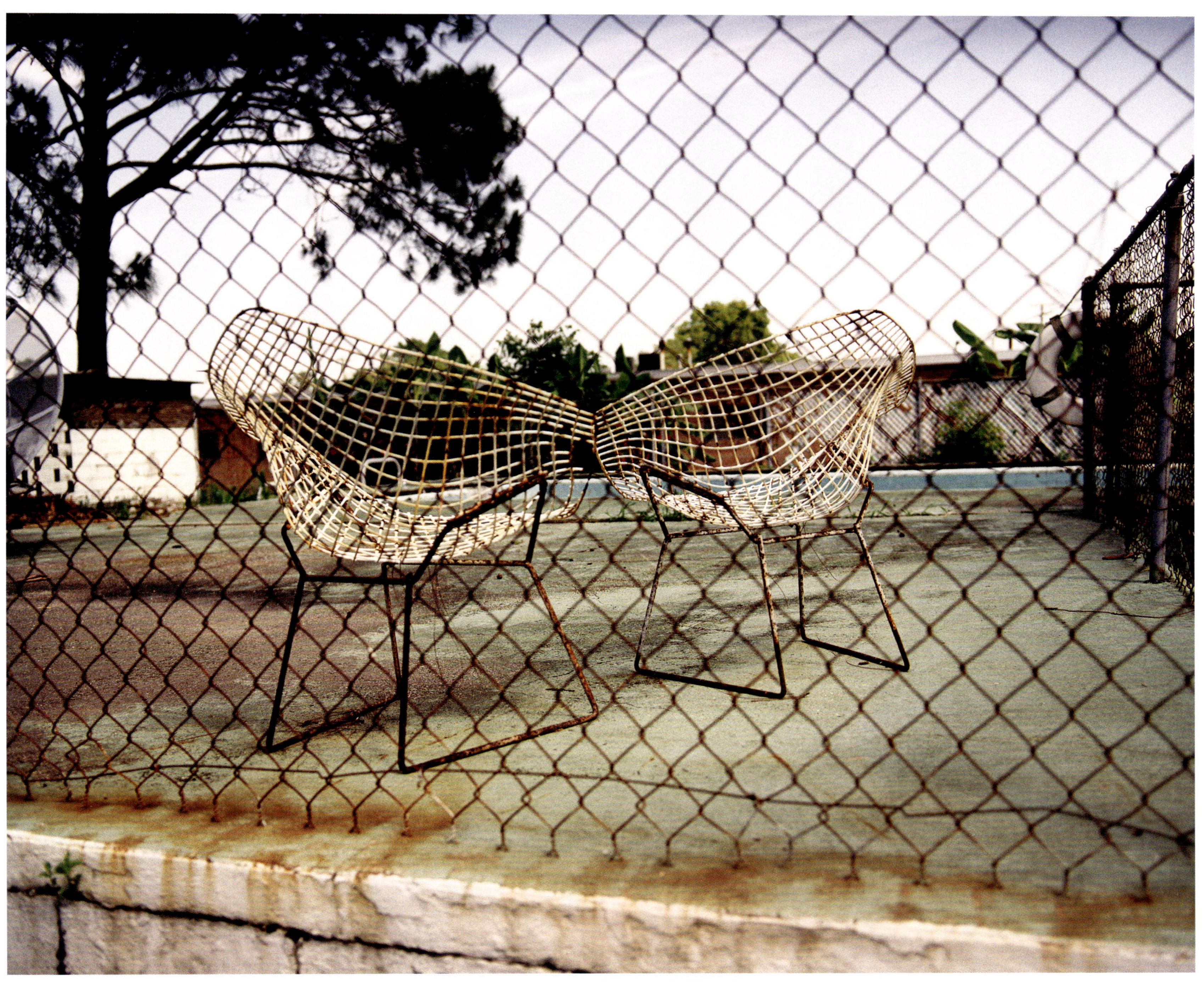

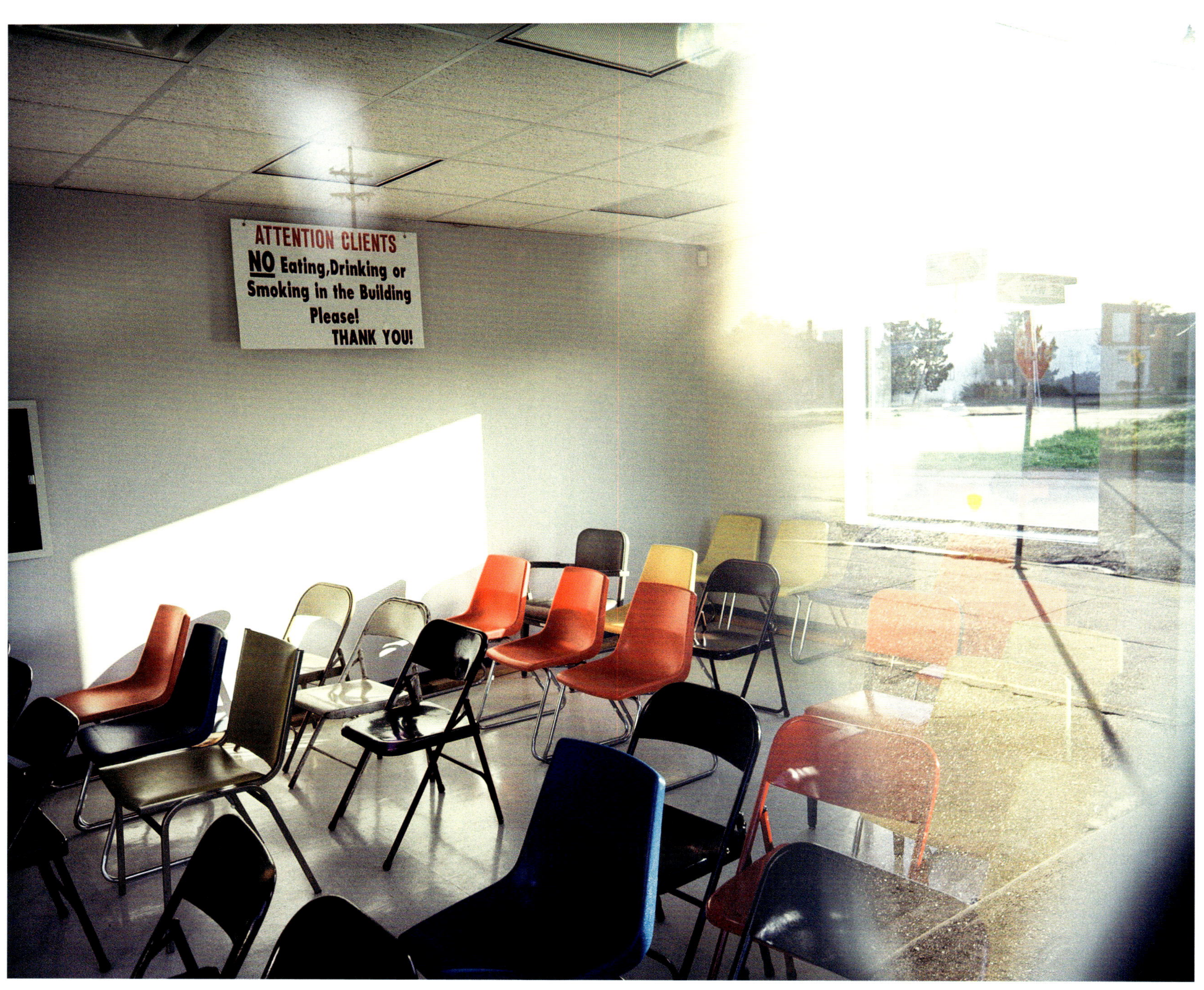
ATTENTION CLIENTS
NO Eating,Drinking or
Smoking in the Building
Please!
THANK YOU!

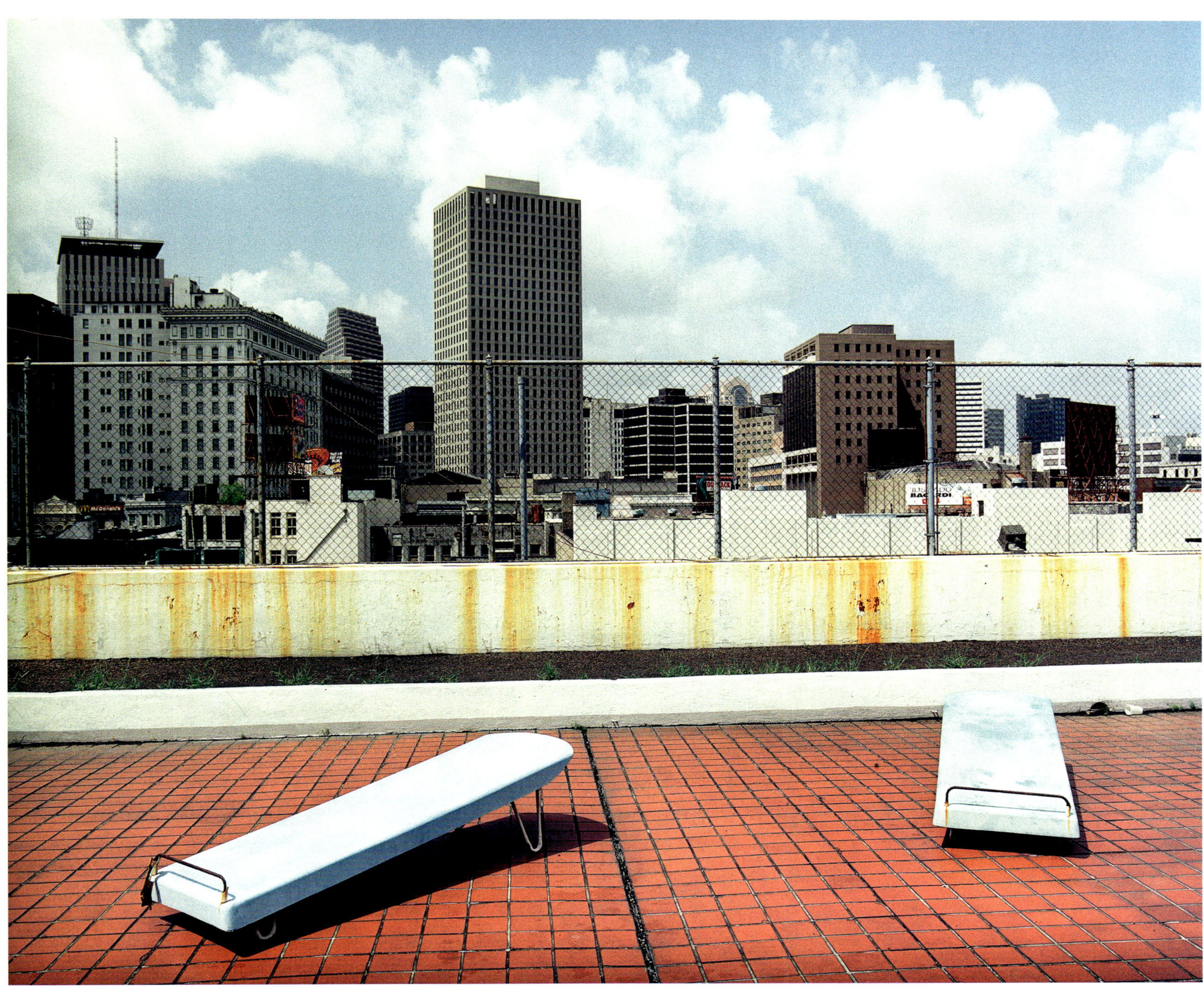

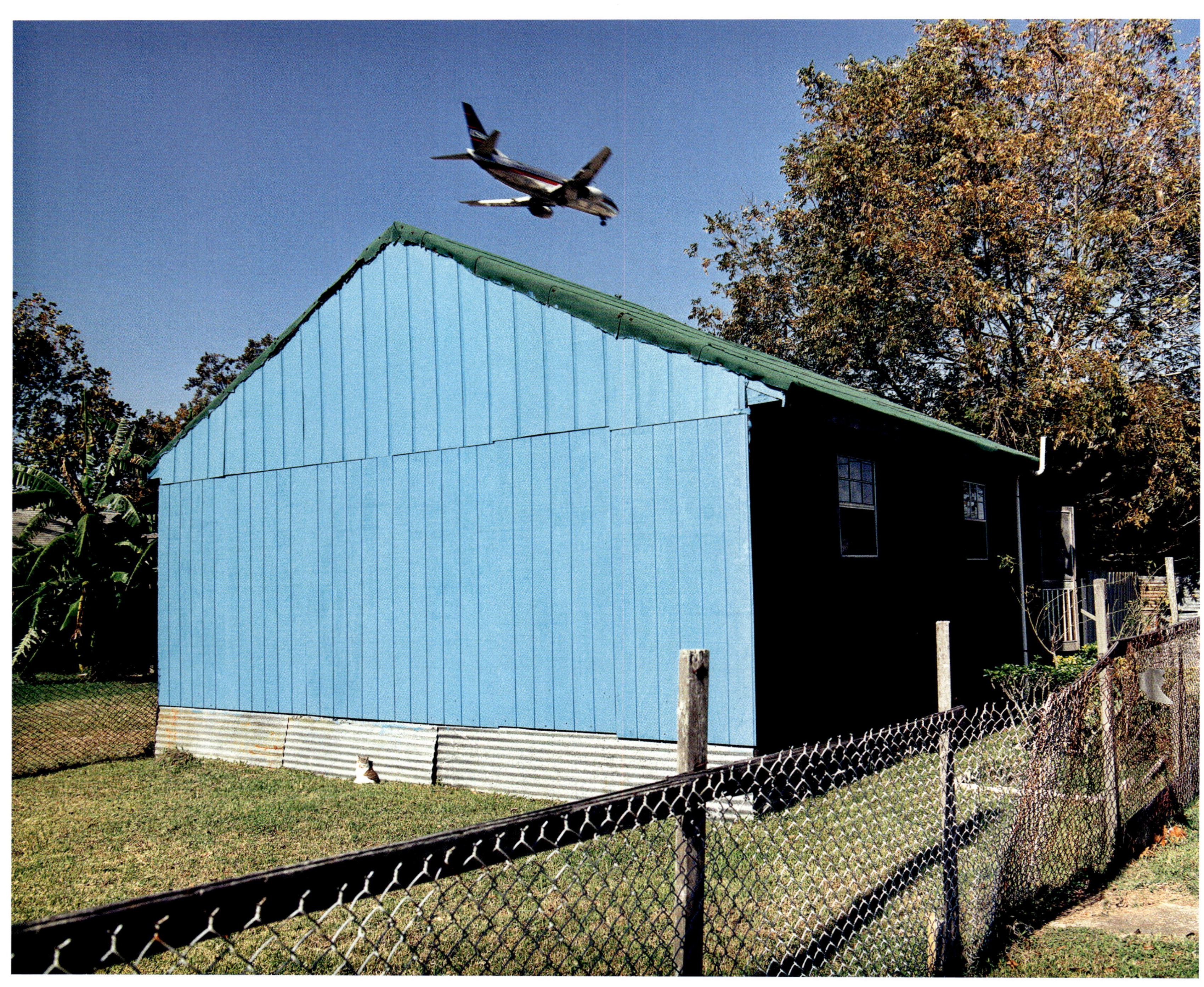

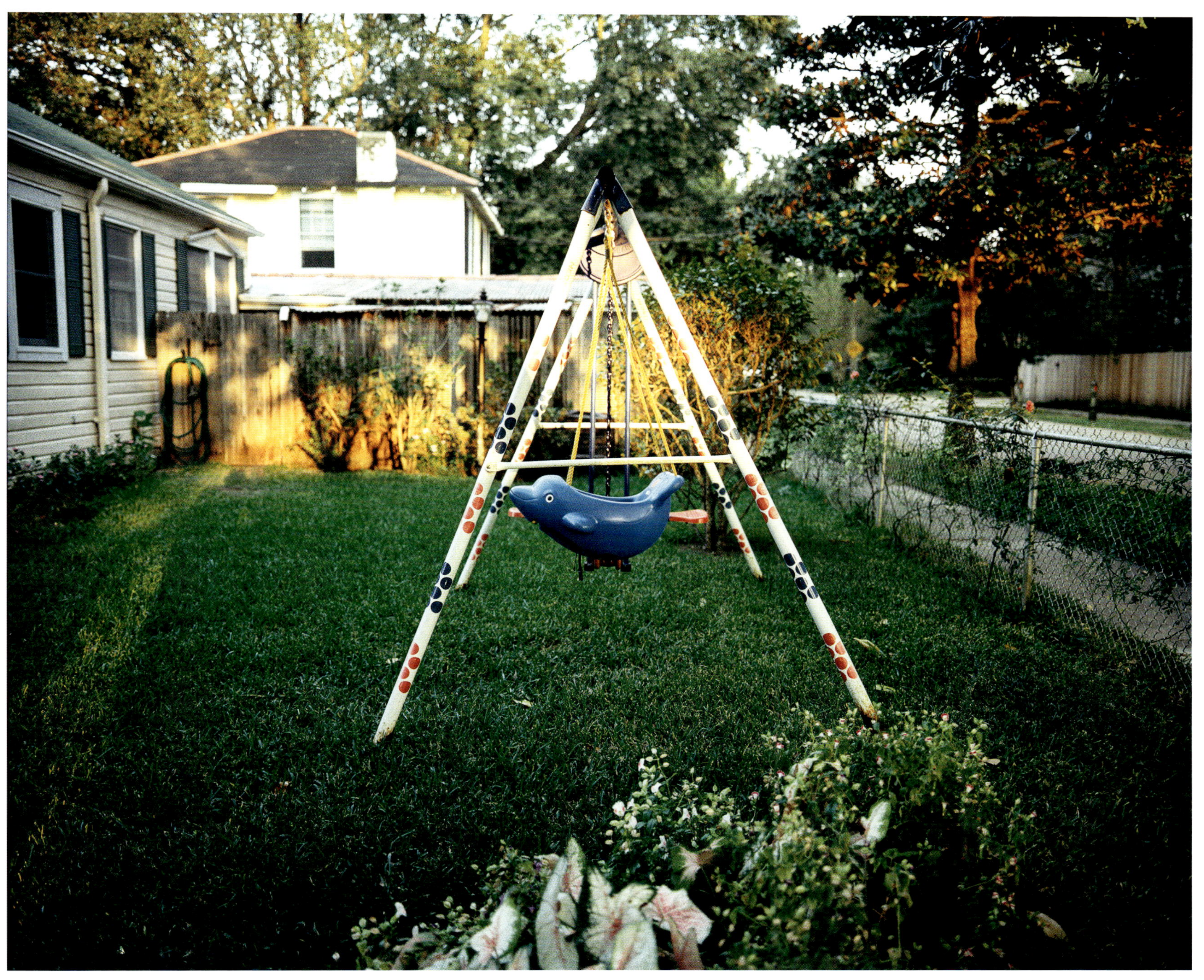

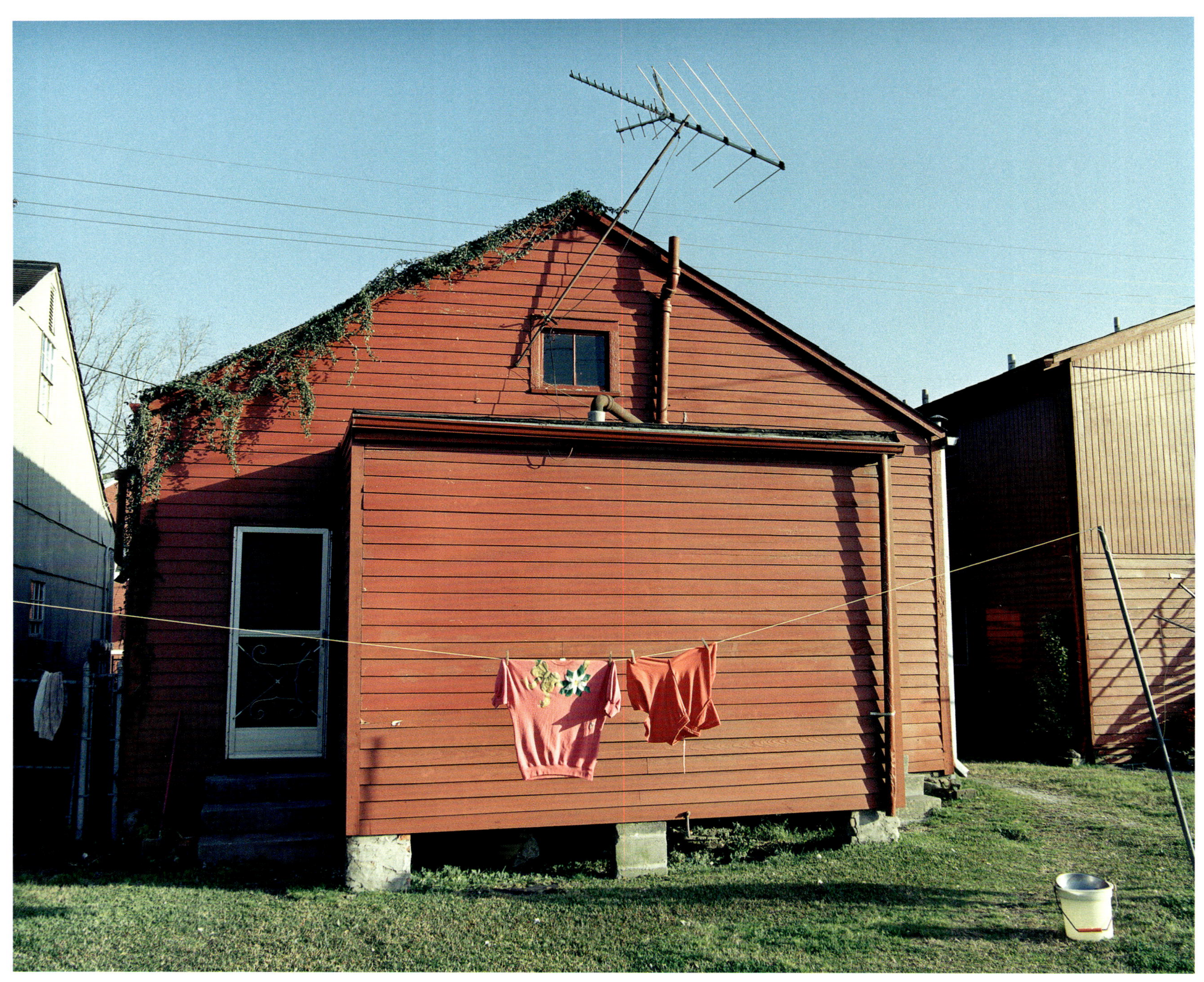

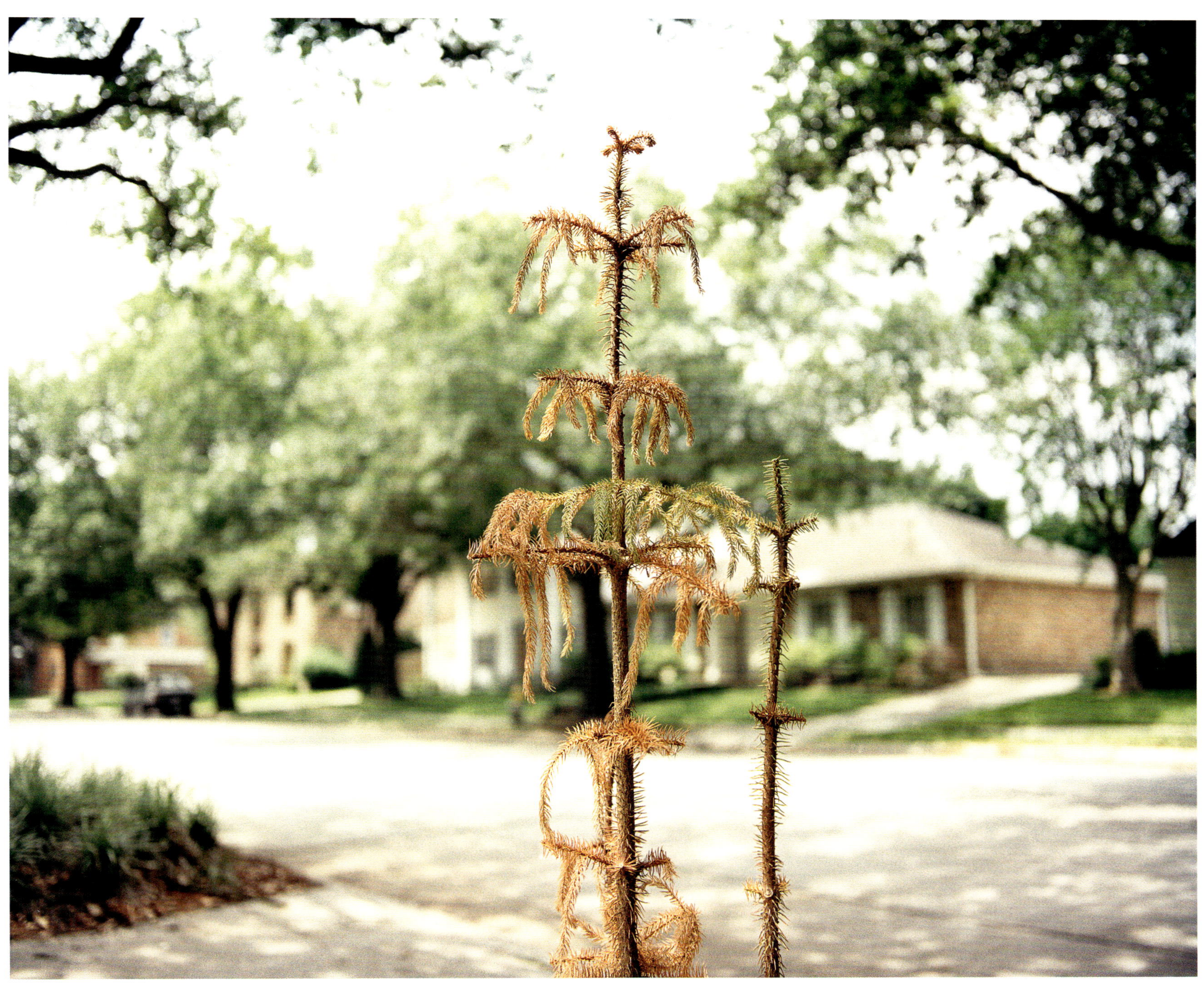

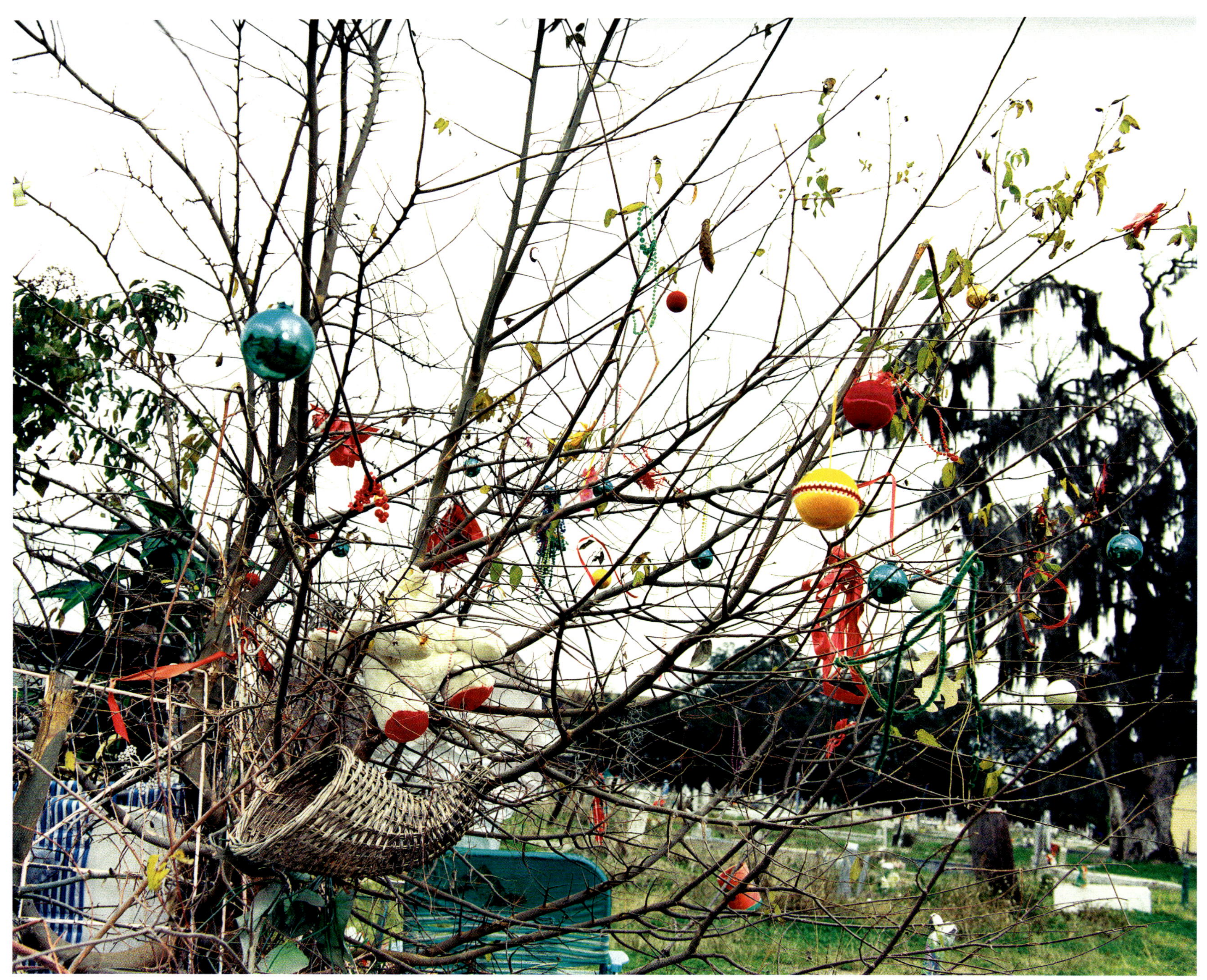

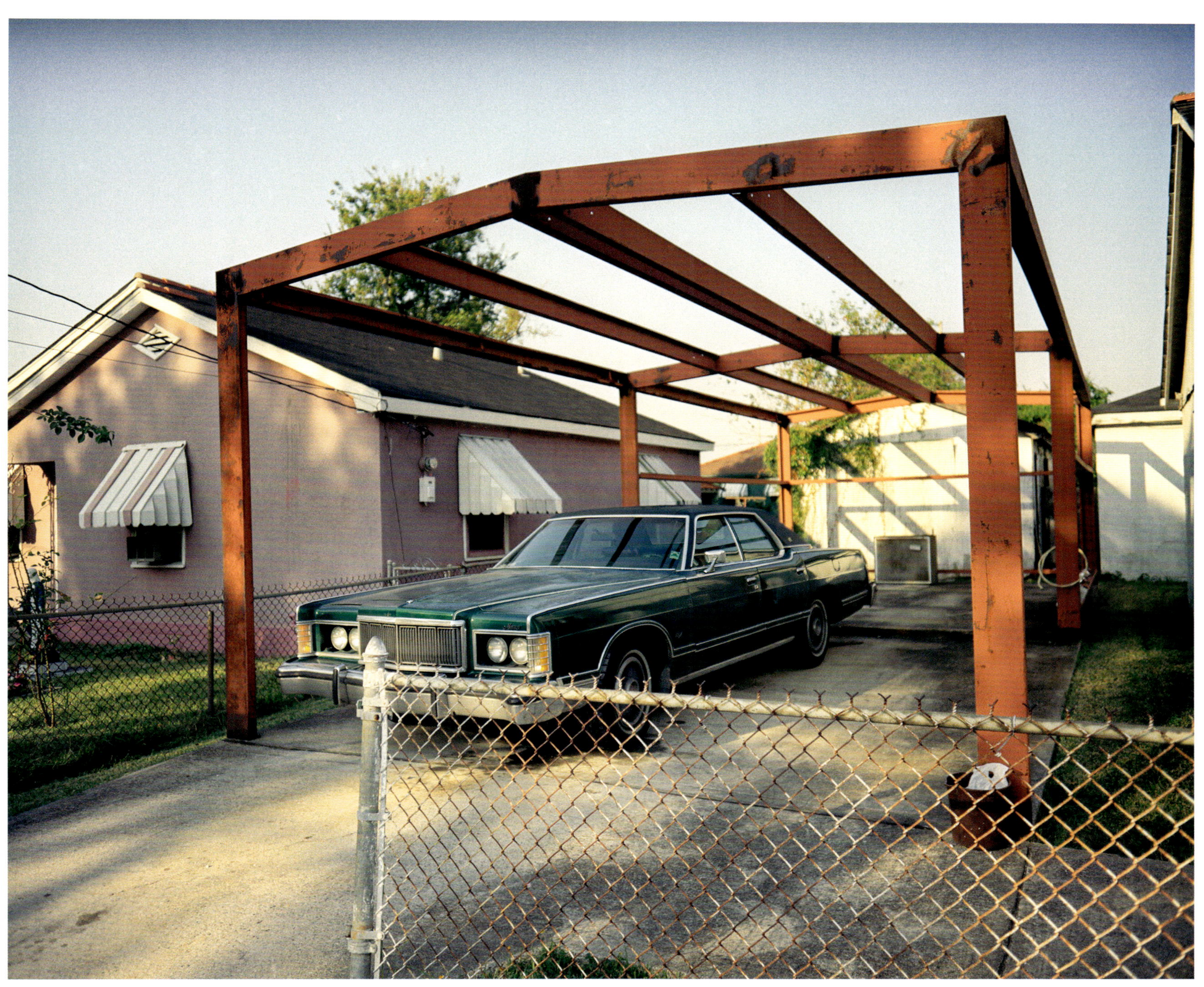

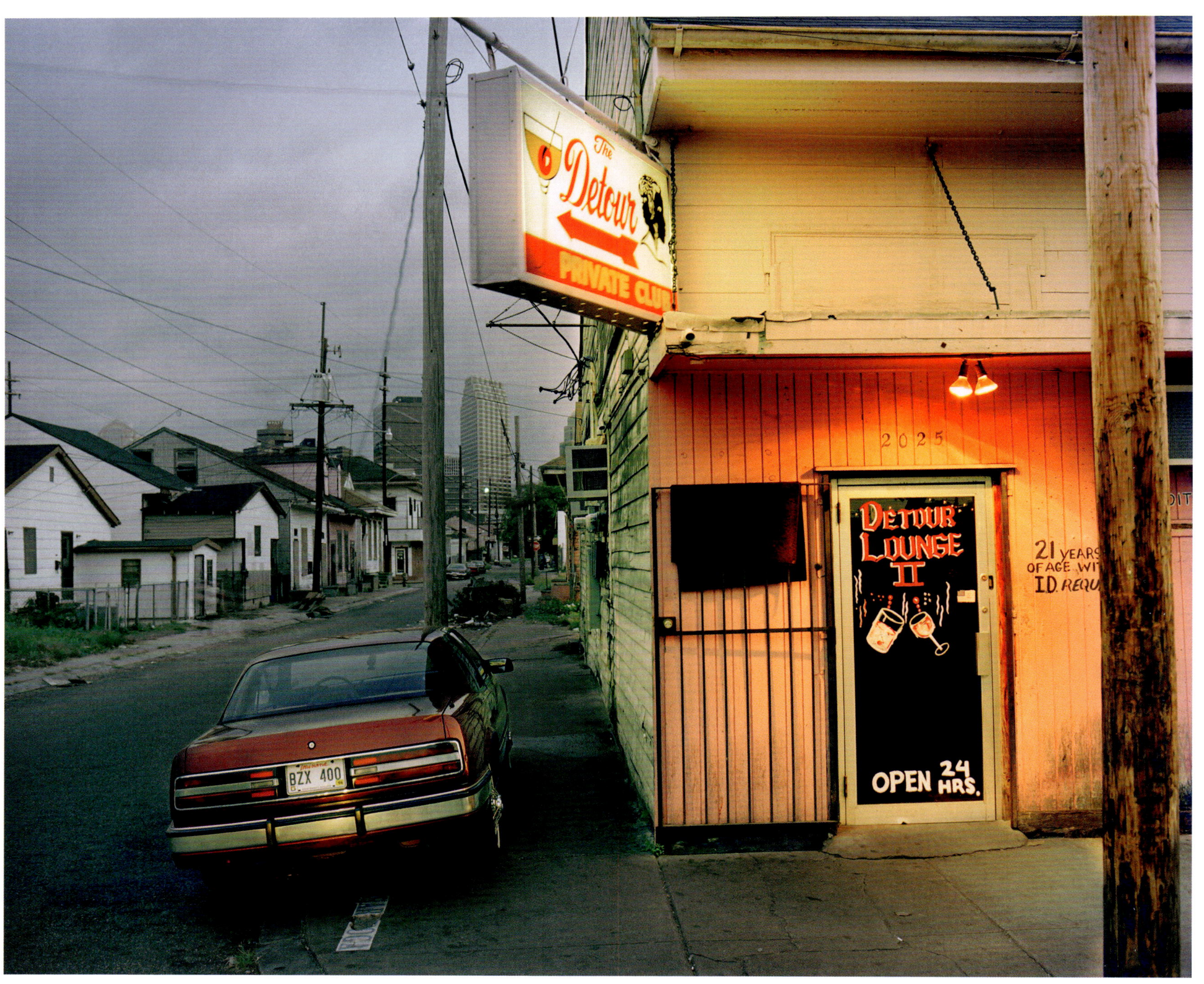
The
Detour
PRIVATE CLUB
2025
DETOUR
LOUNGE
II
OPEN 24 HRS.
21 YEARS
OF AGE WIT
I.D. REQU
BZX 400

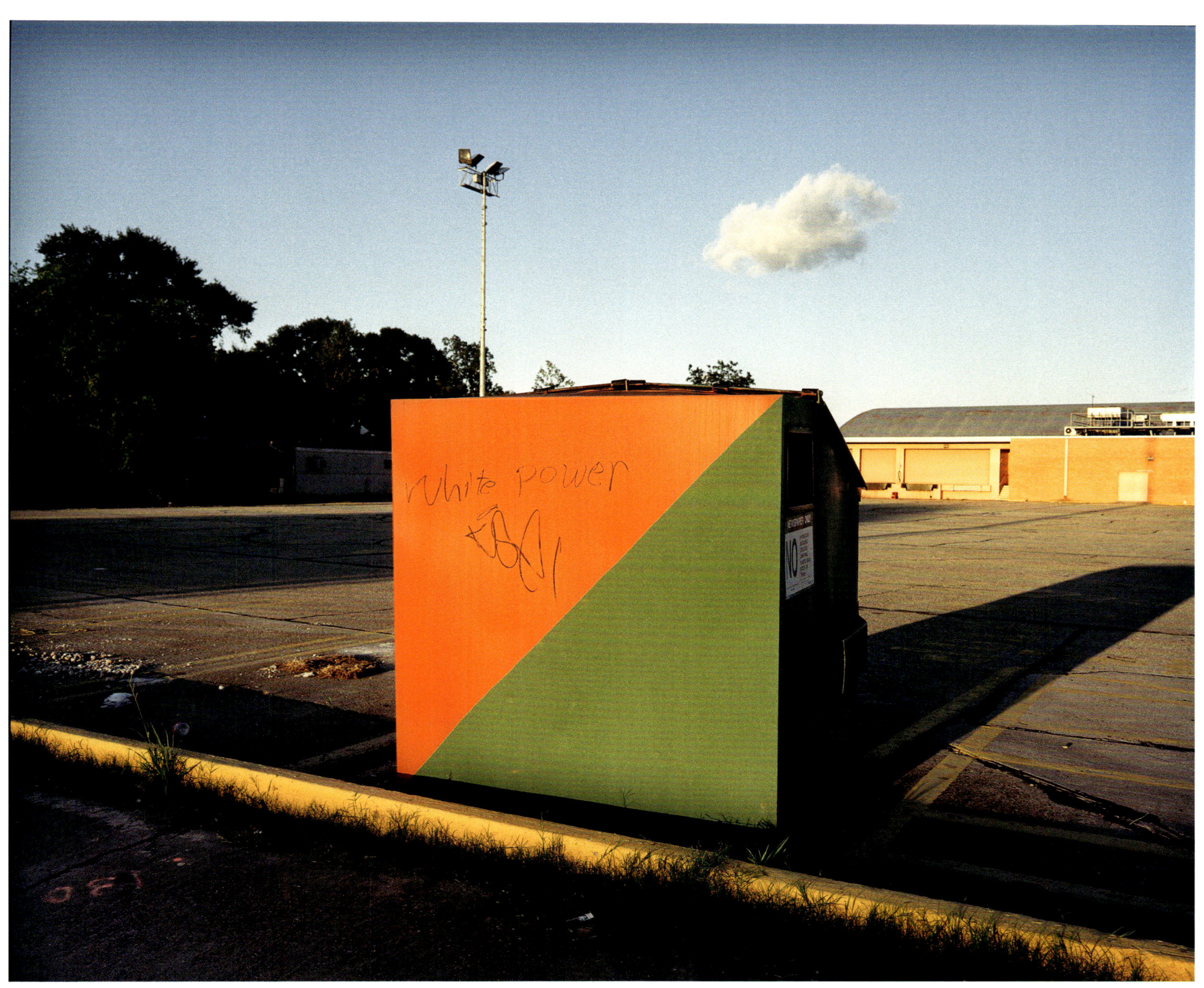
White power

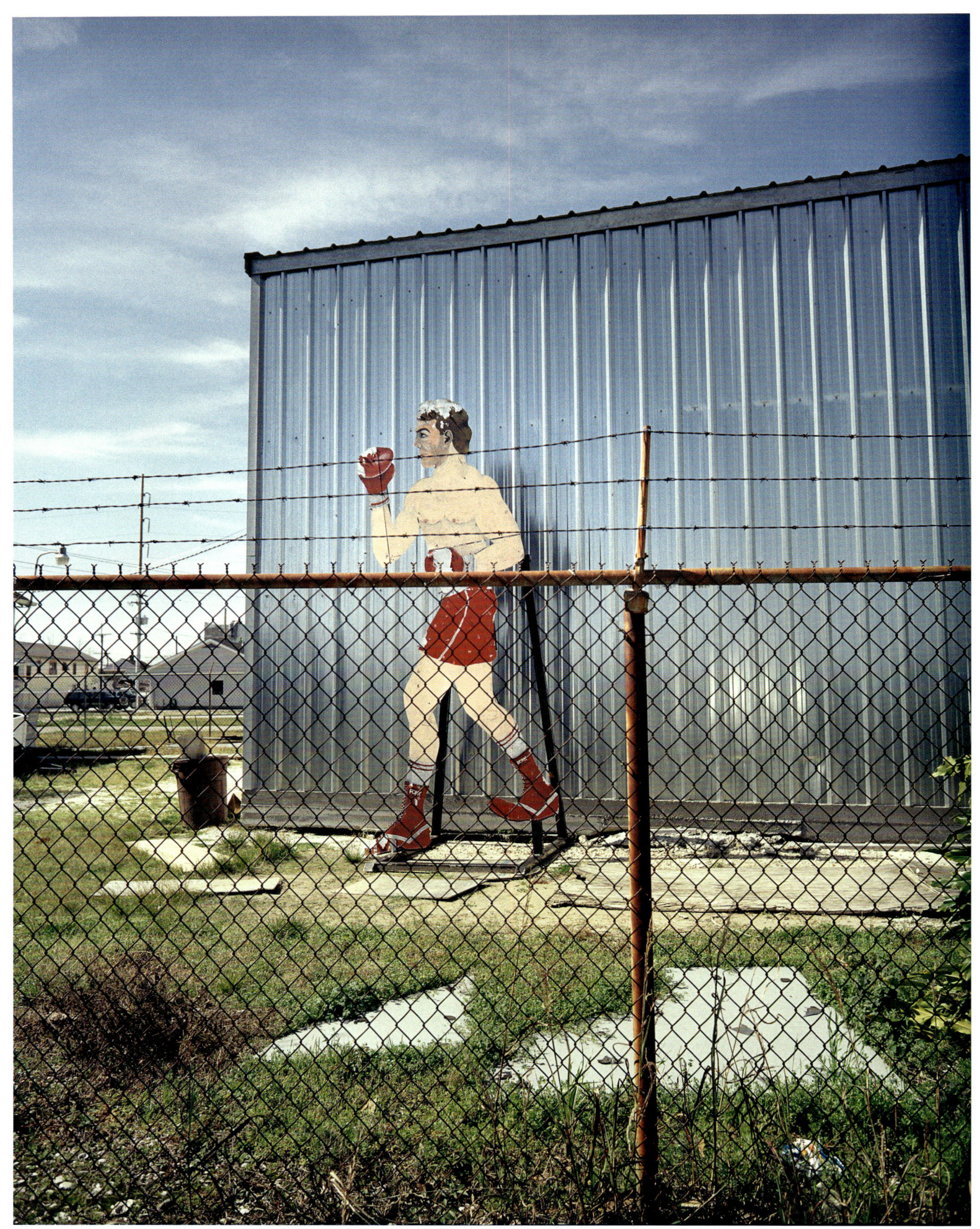

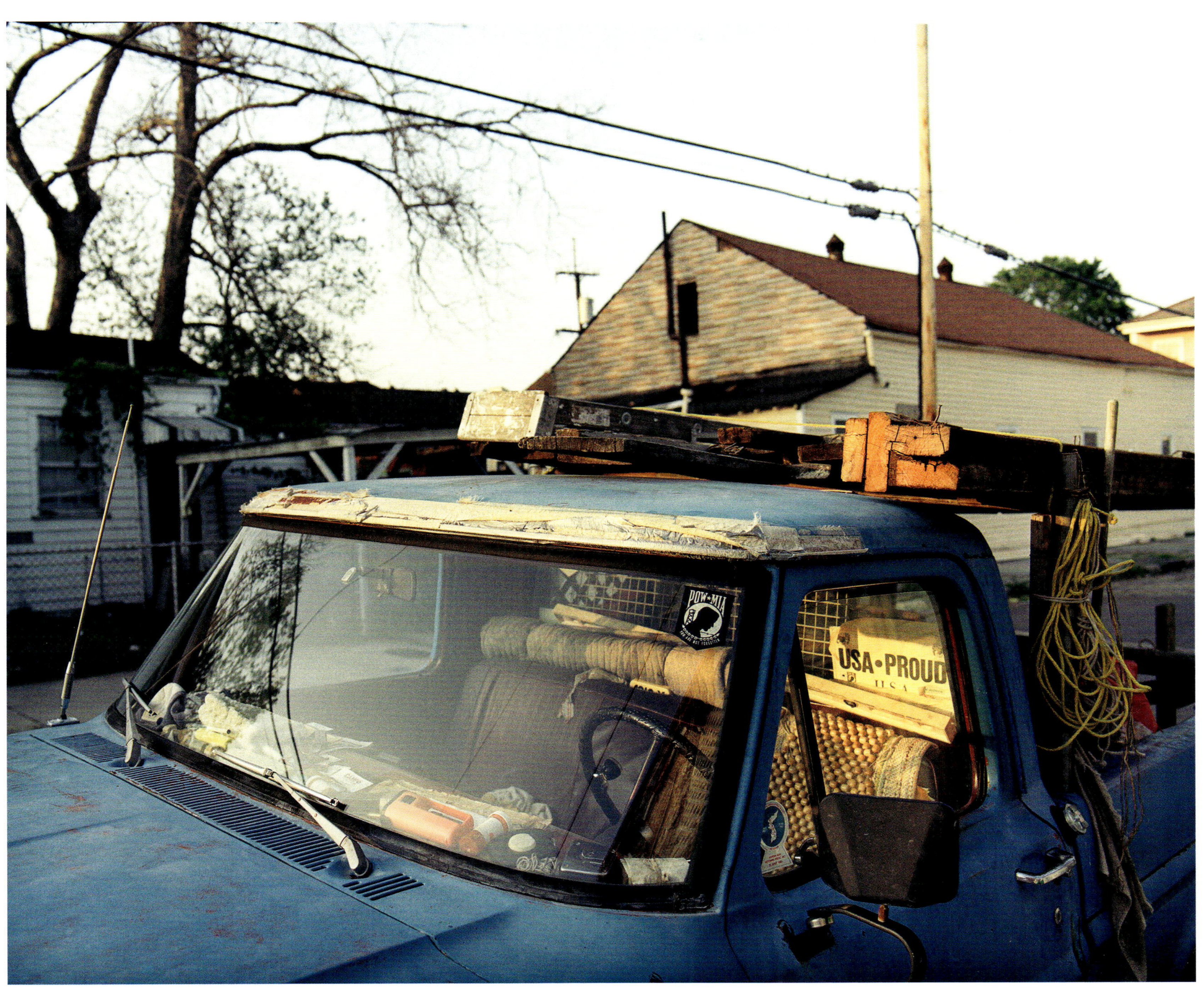
POW·MIA
USA·PROUD

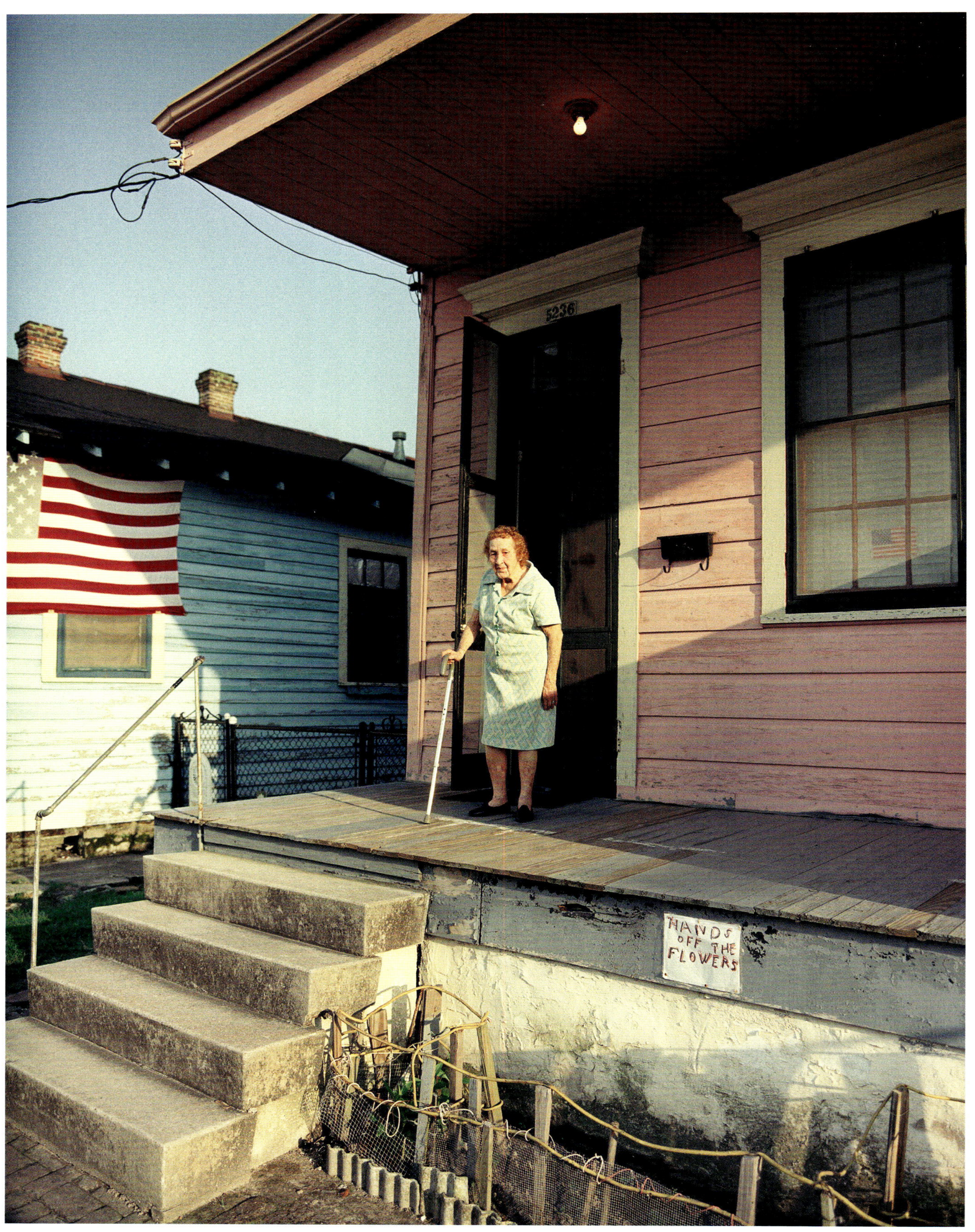
5236
HANDS
OFF THE
FLOWERS

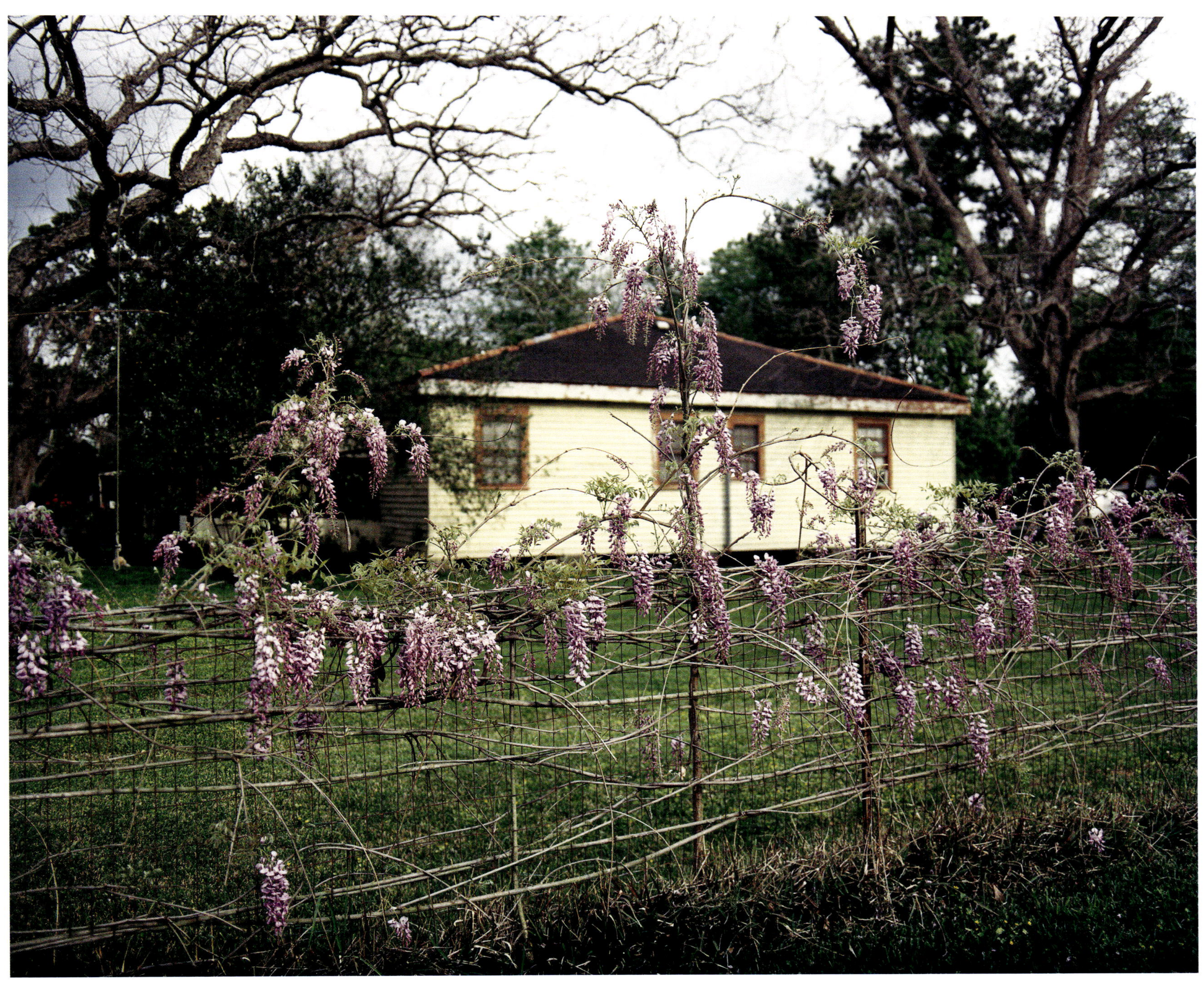

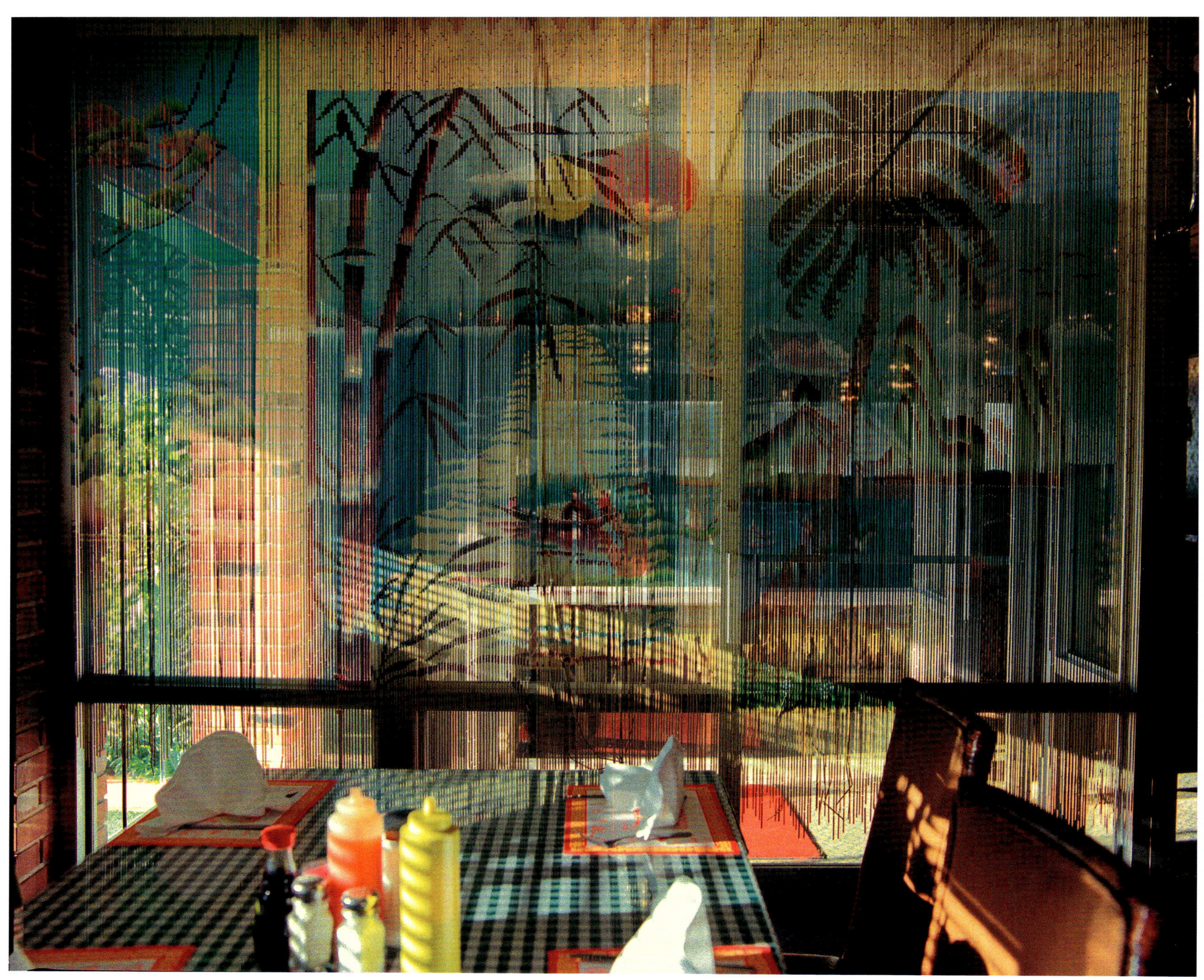

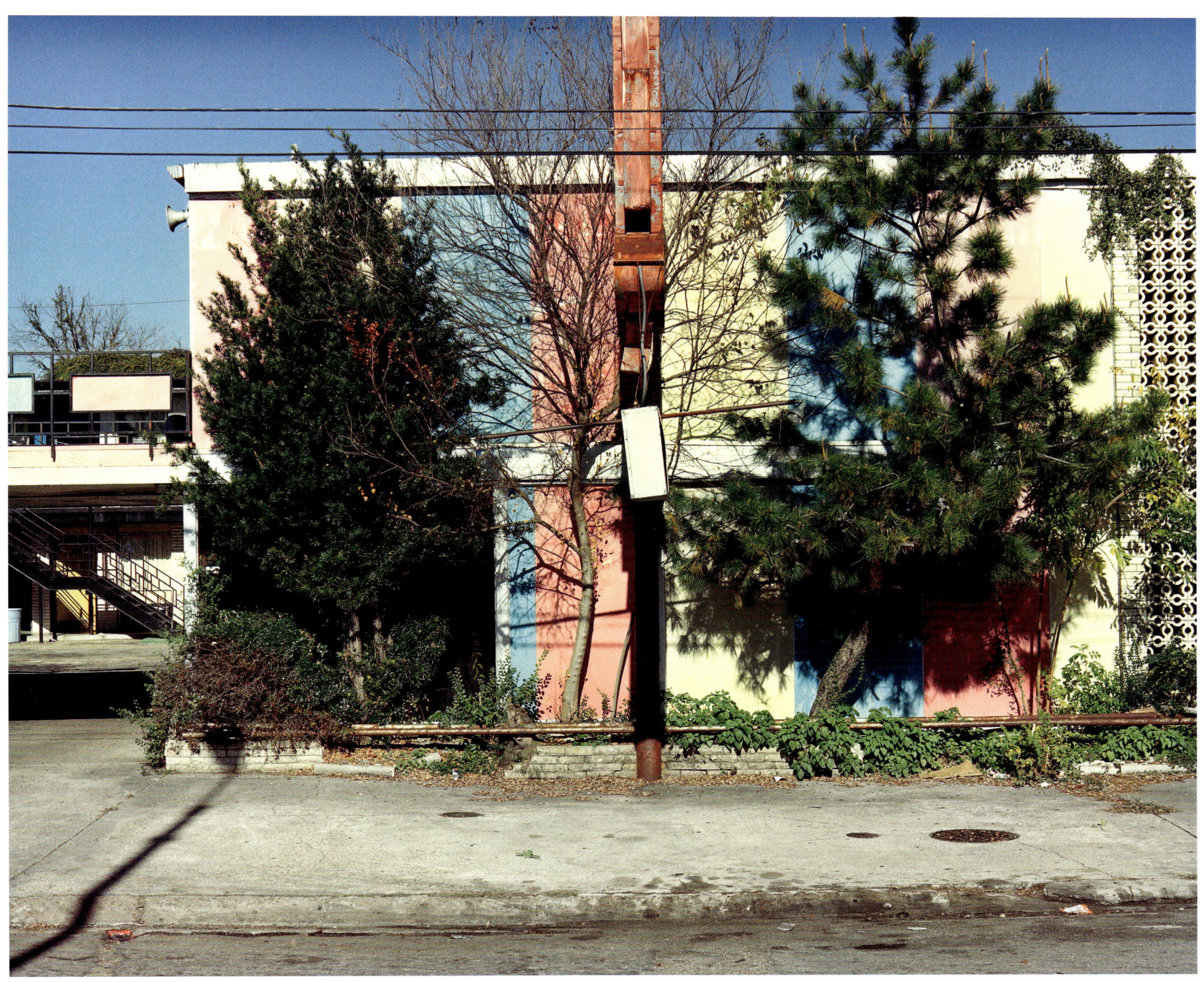

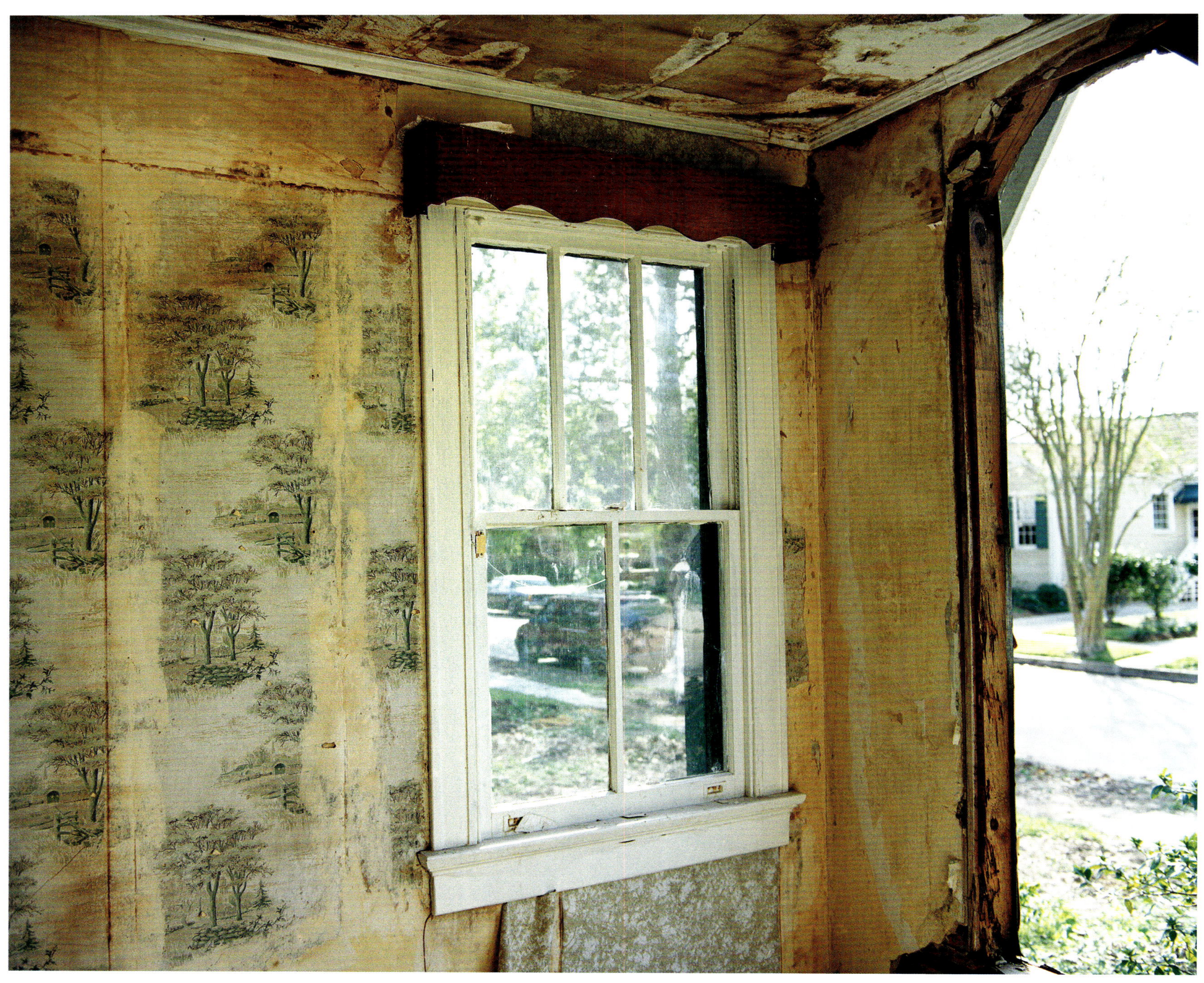

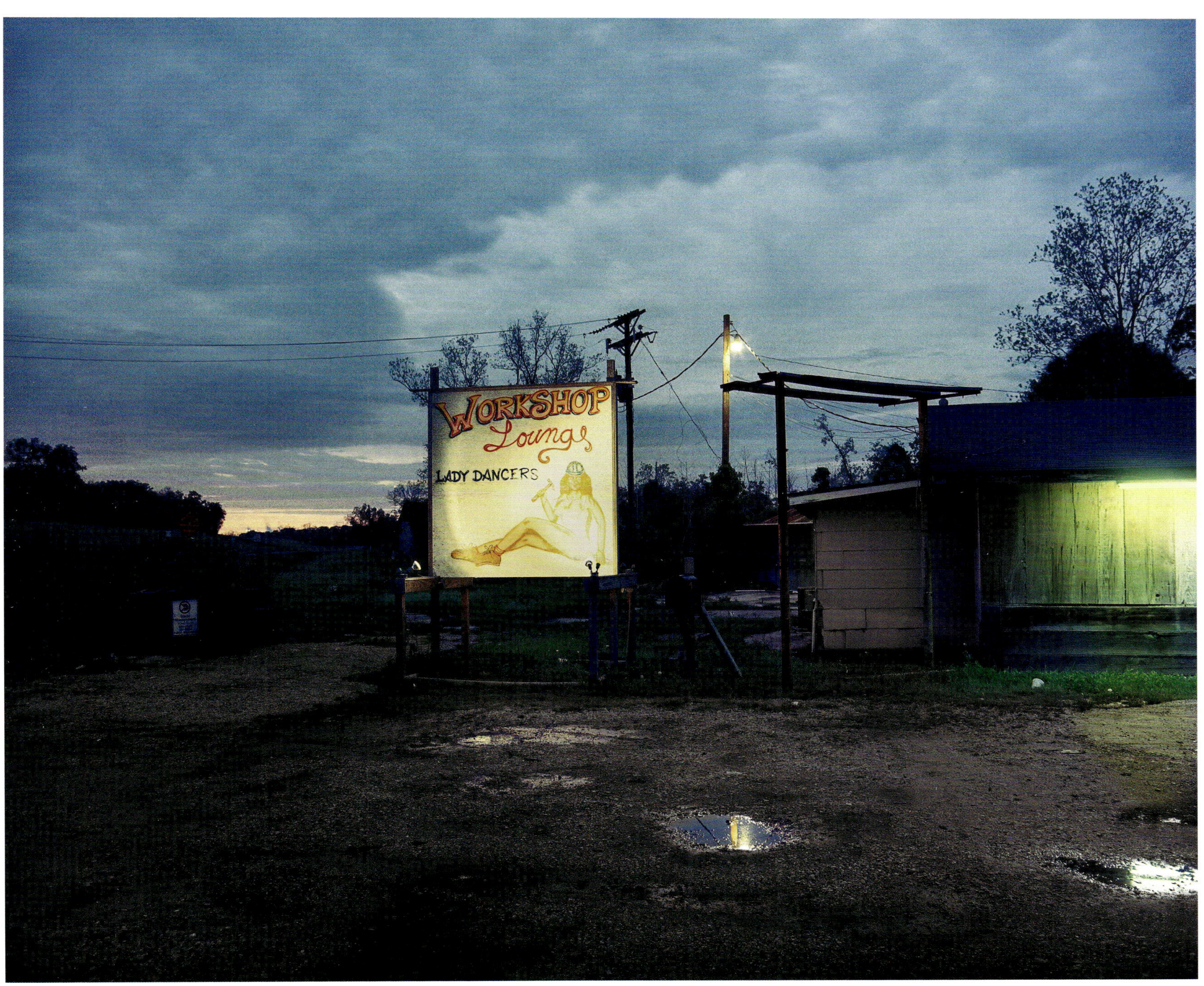
WORKSHOP
Lounge
LADY DANCERS

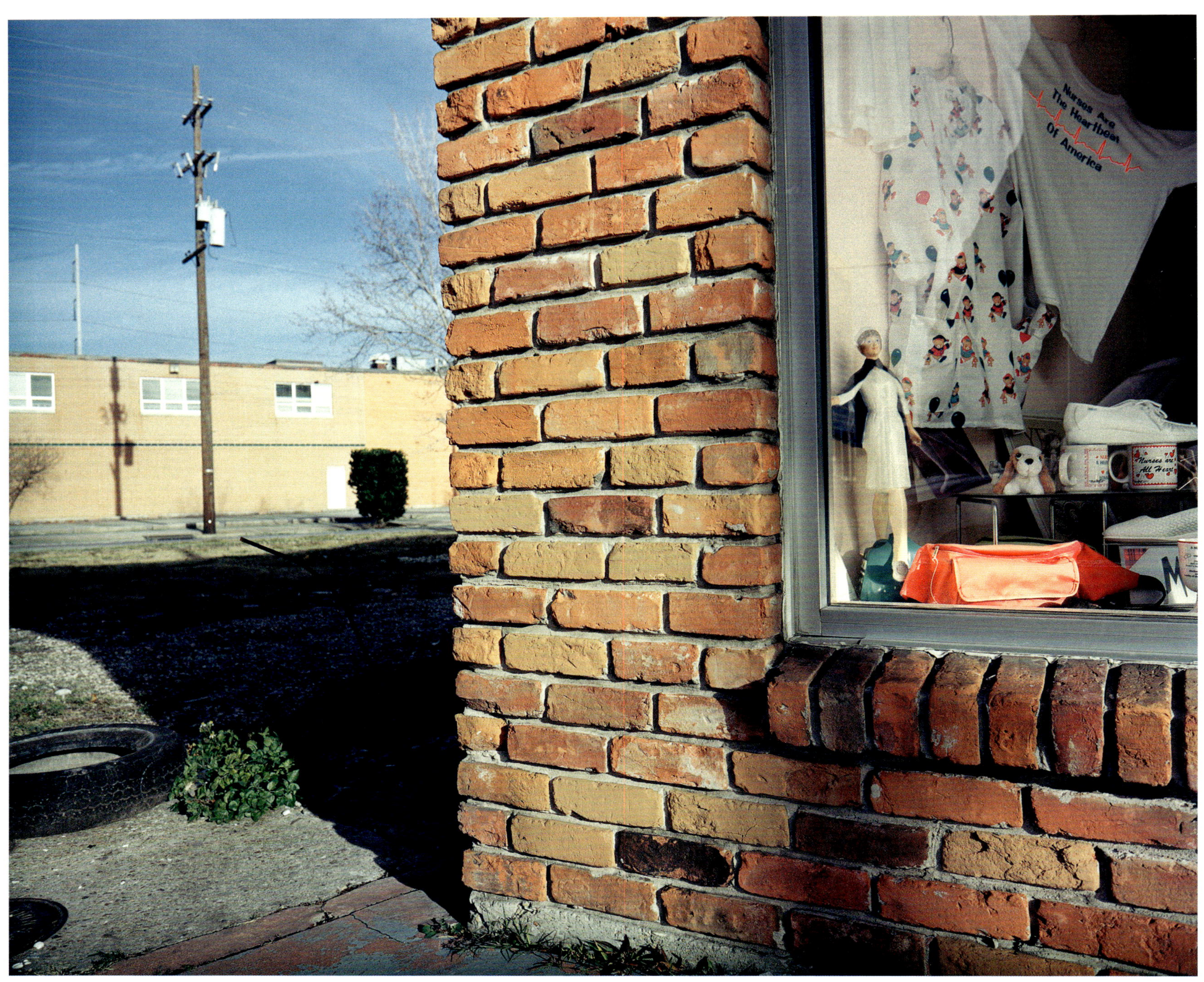
Nurses Are
The Heartbeat
Of America
Nurses are
All Heart

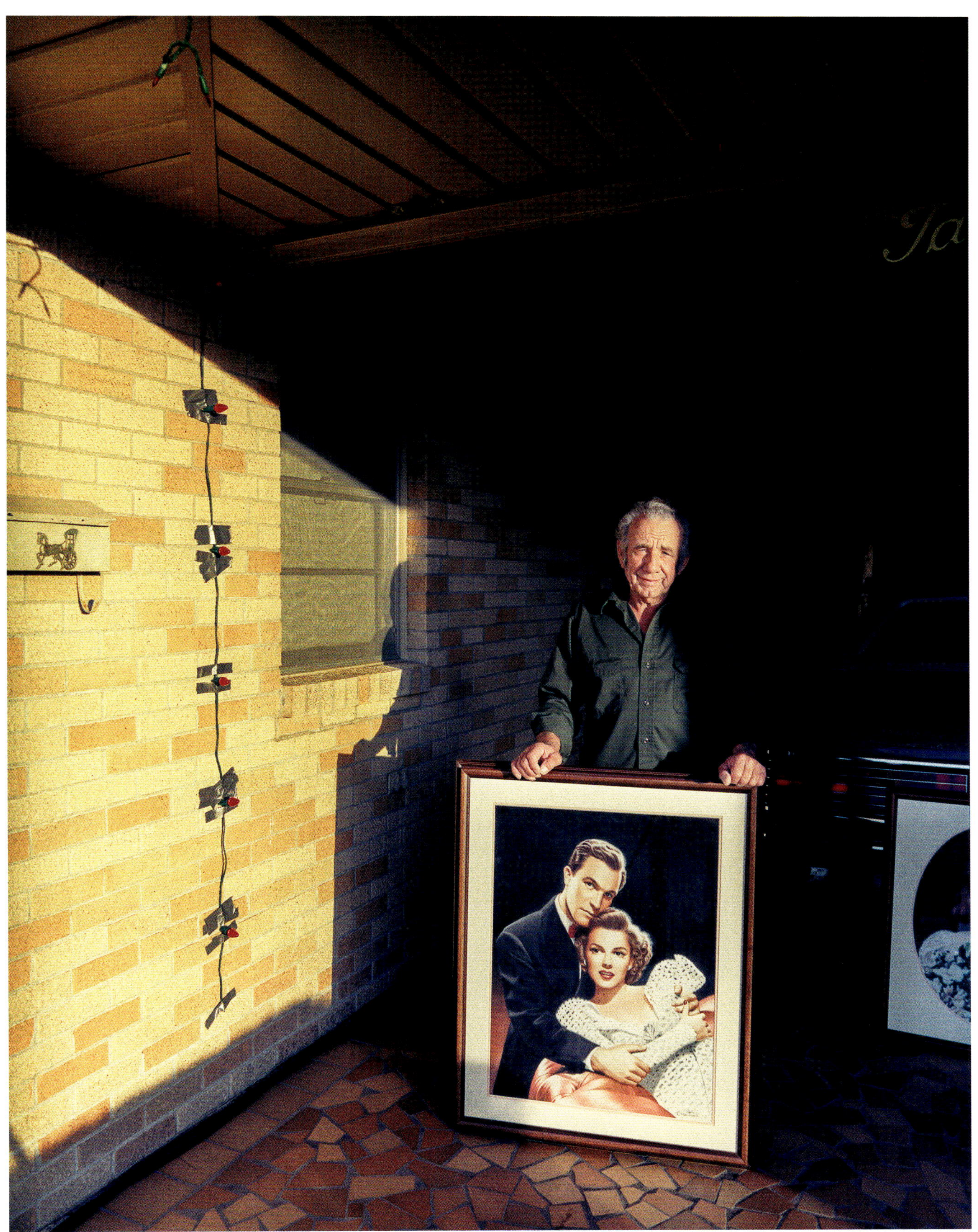

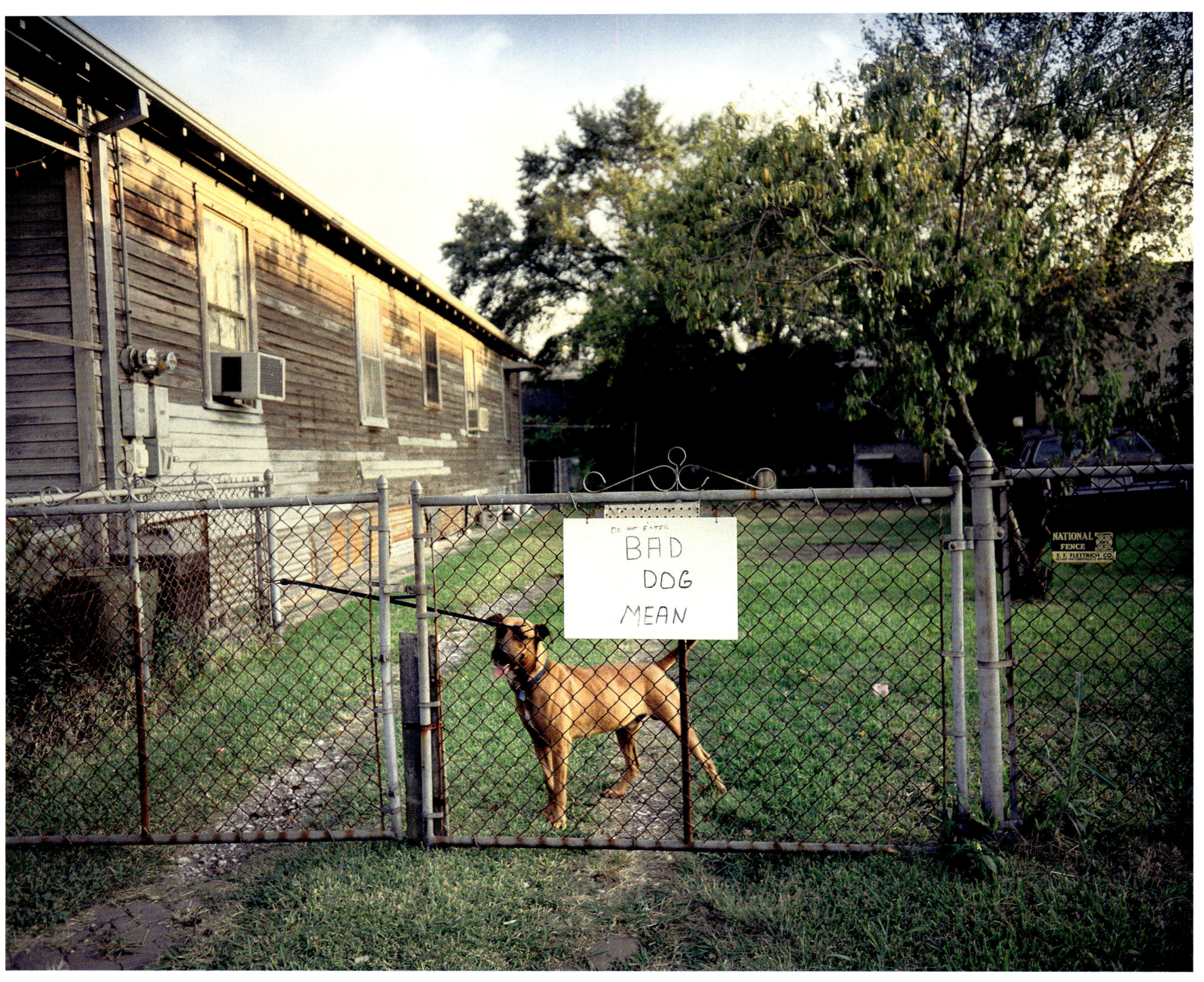
DO NOT ENTER
BAD
DOG
MEAN
NATIONAL
FENCE
E. F. FLETTRICH CO.

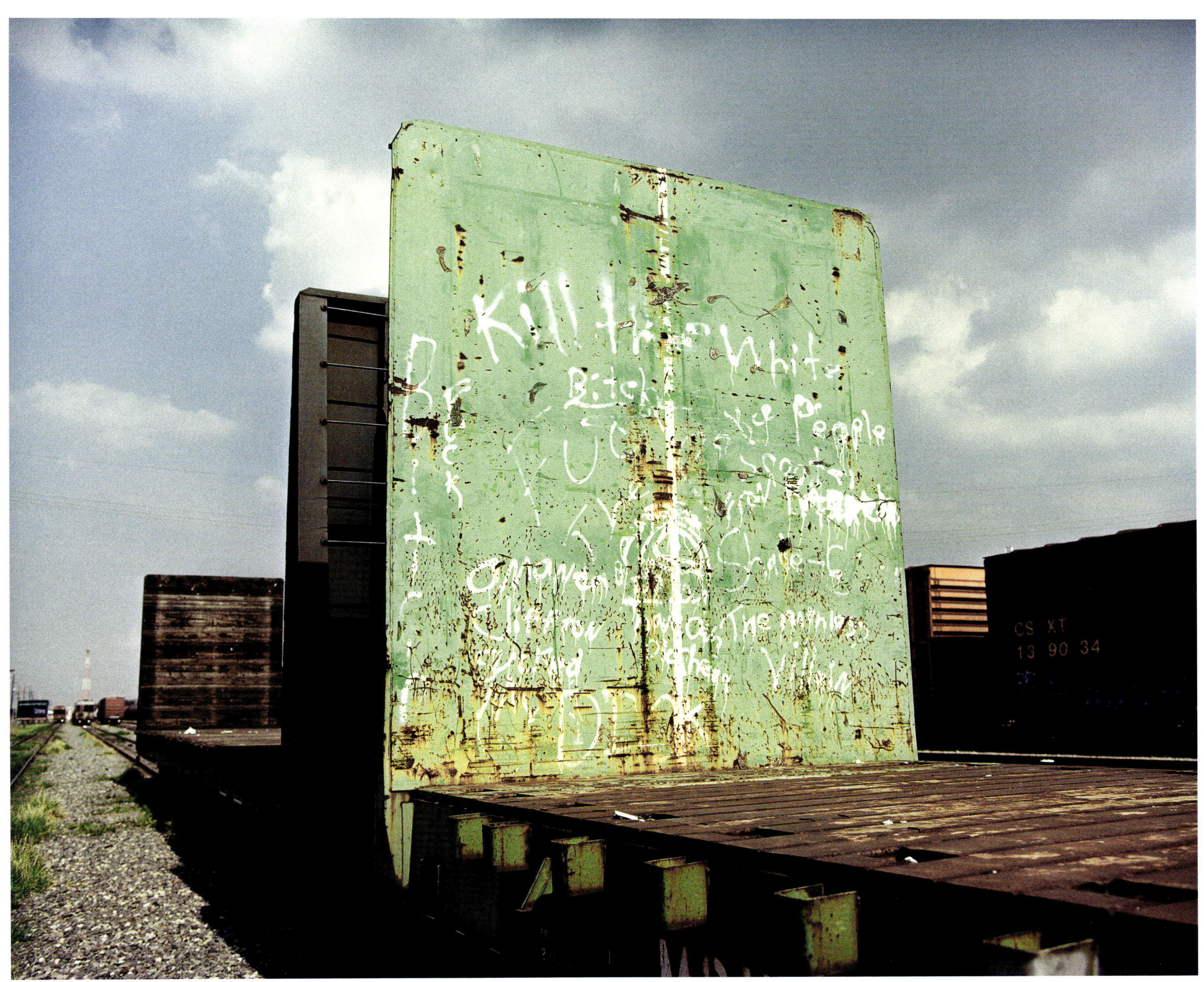
CS XT
13 90 34

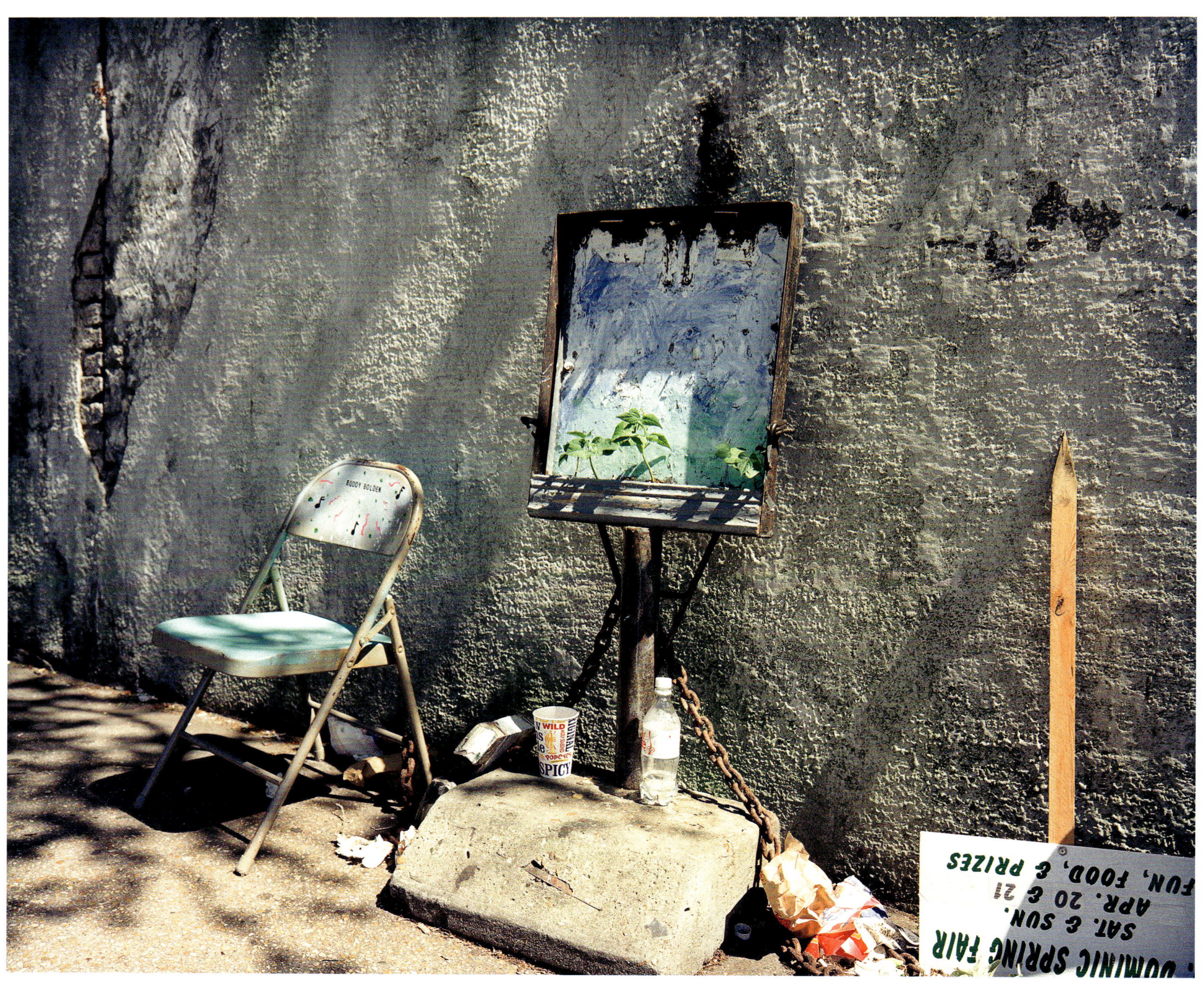
BUDDY BOLDEN
WILD
SPICY
DOMINIC SPRING FAIR
SAT. & SUN.
APR. 20 & 21
FUN, FOOD, & PRIZES

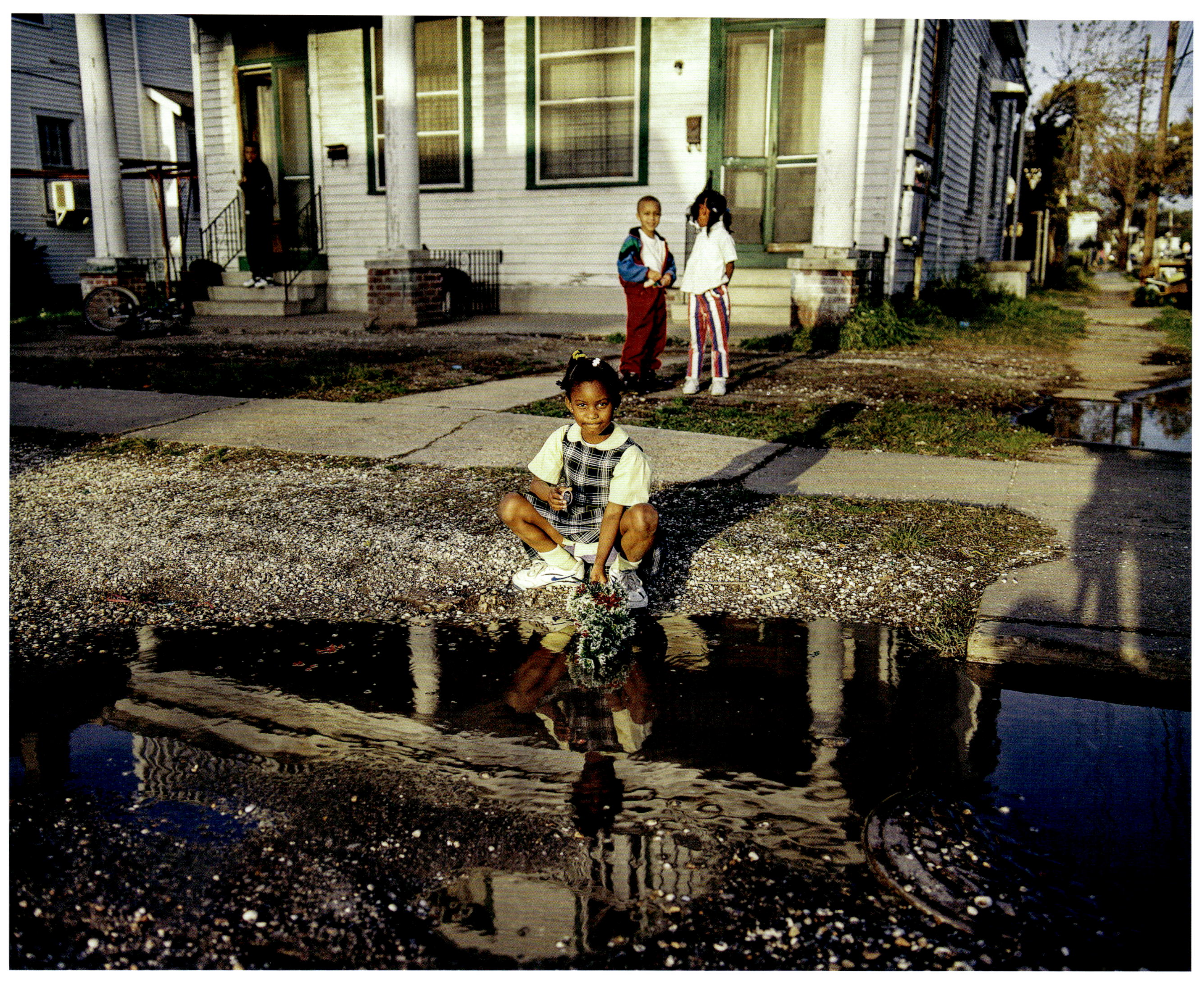

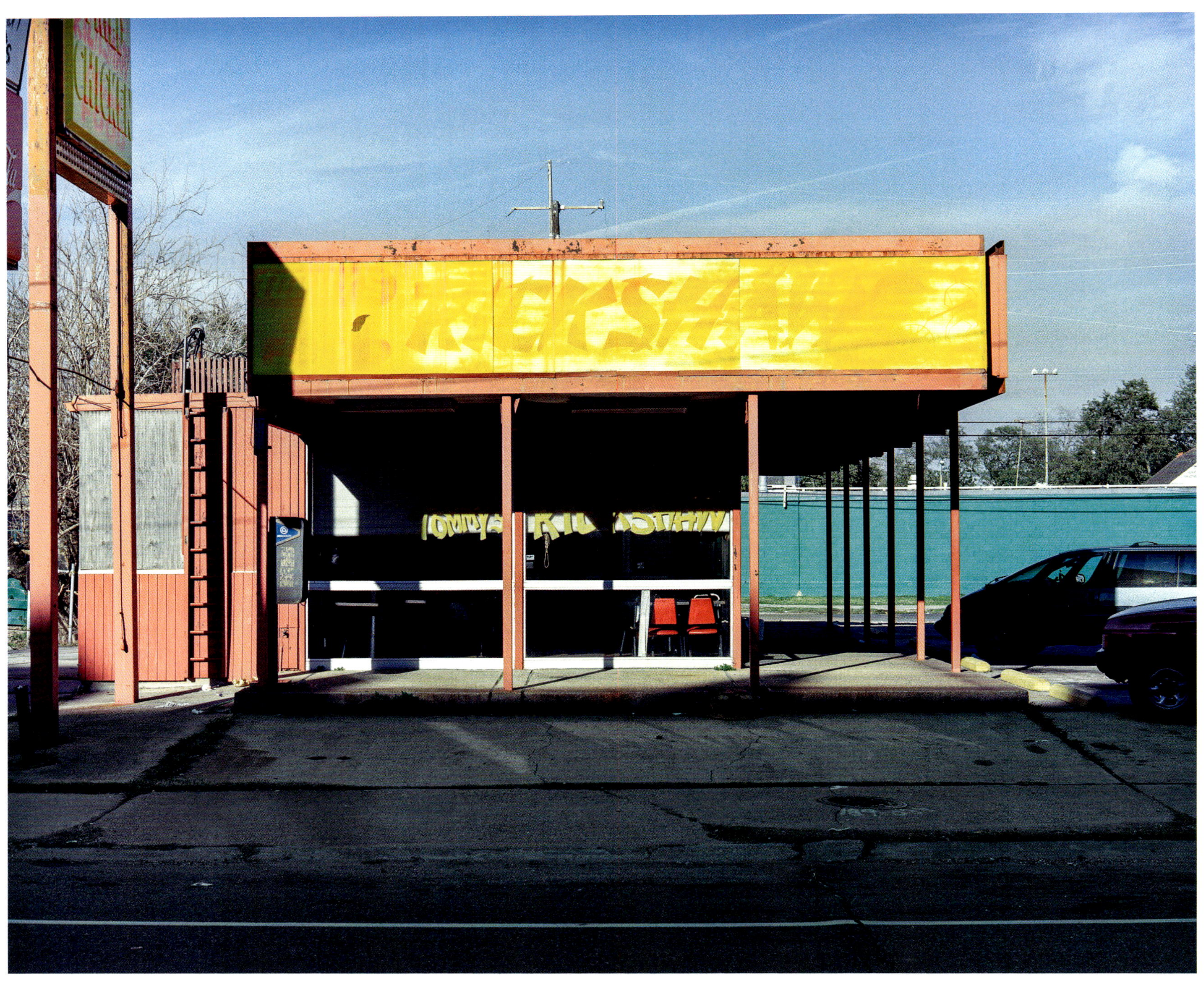
CHICKEN

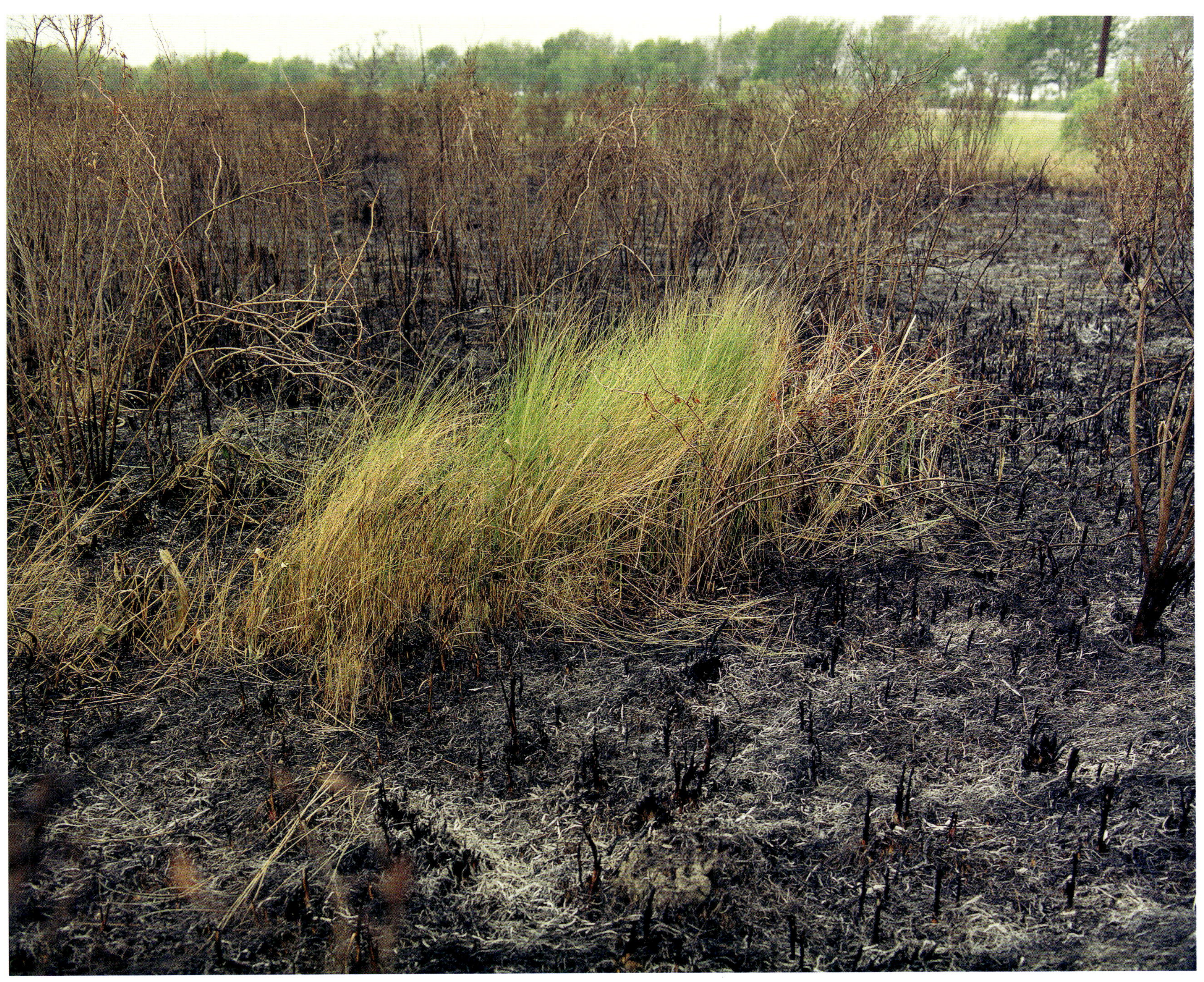

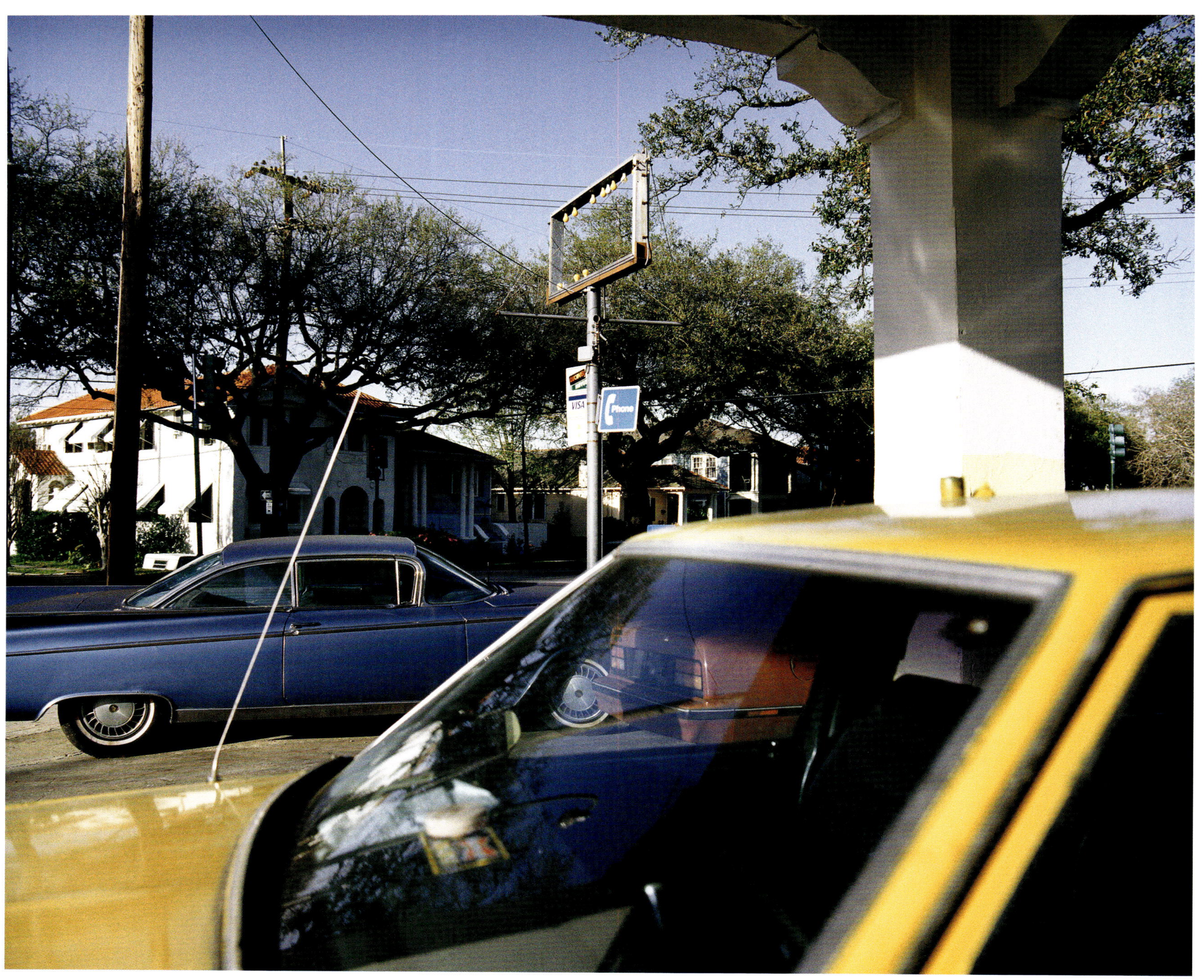
VISA
Phone

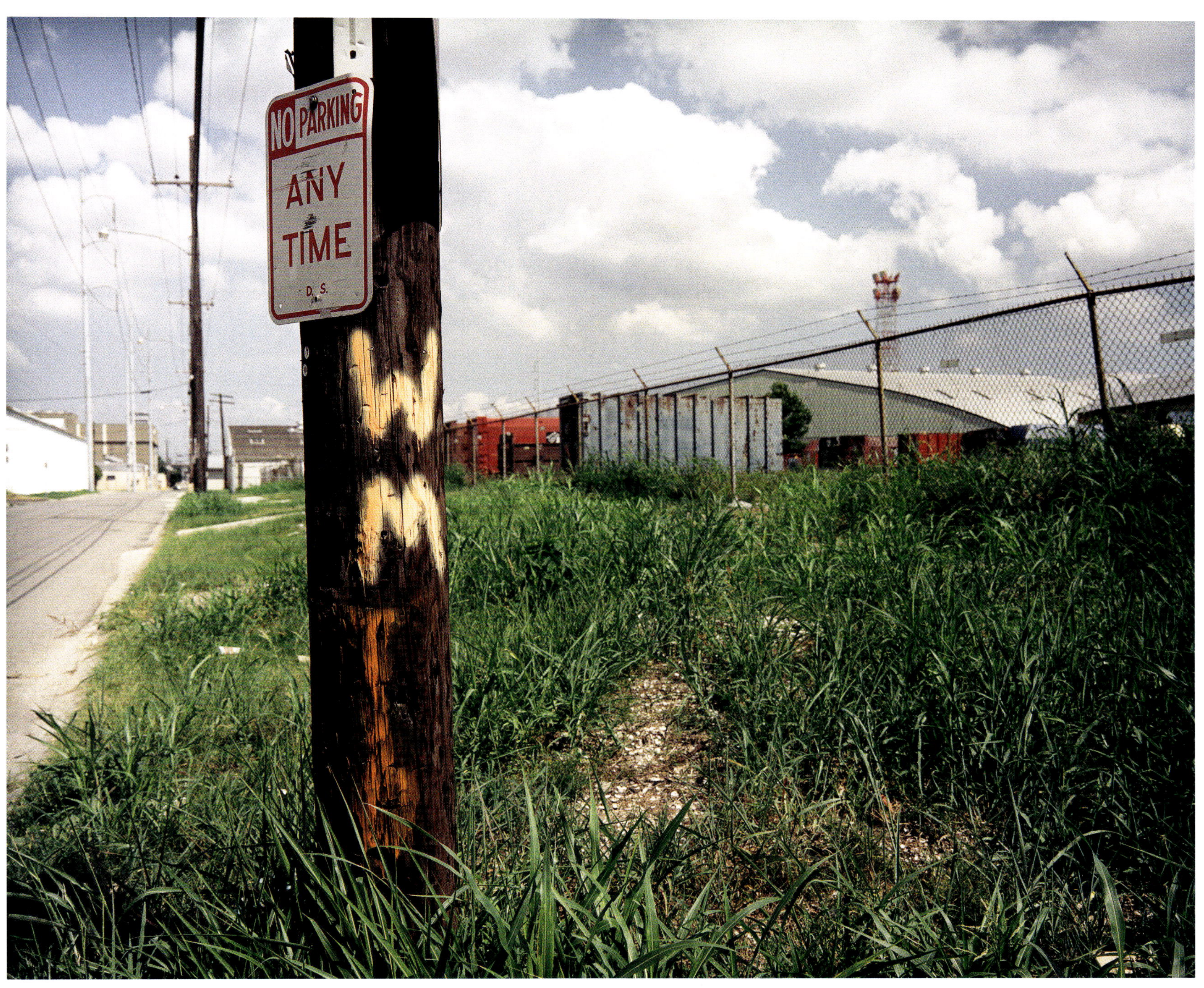
NO PARKING
ANY
TIME
D. S.

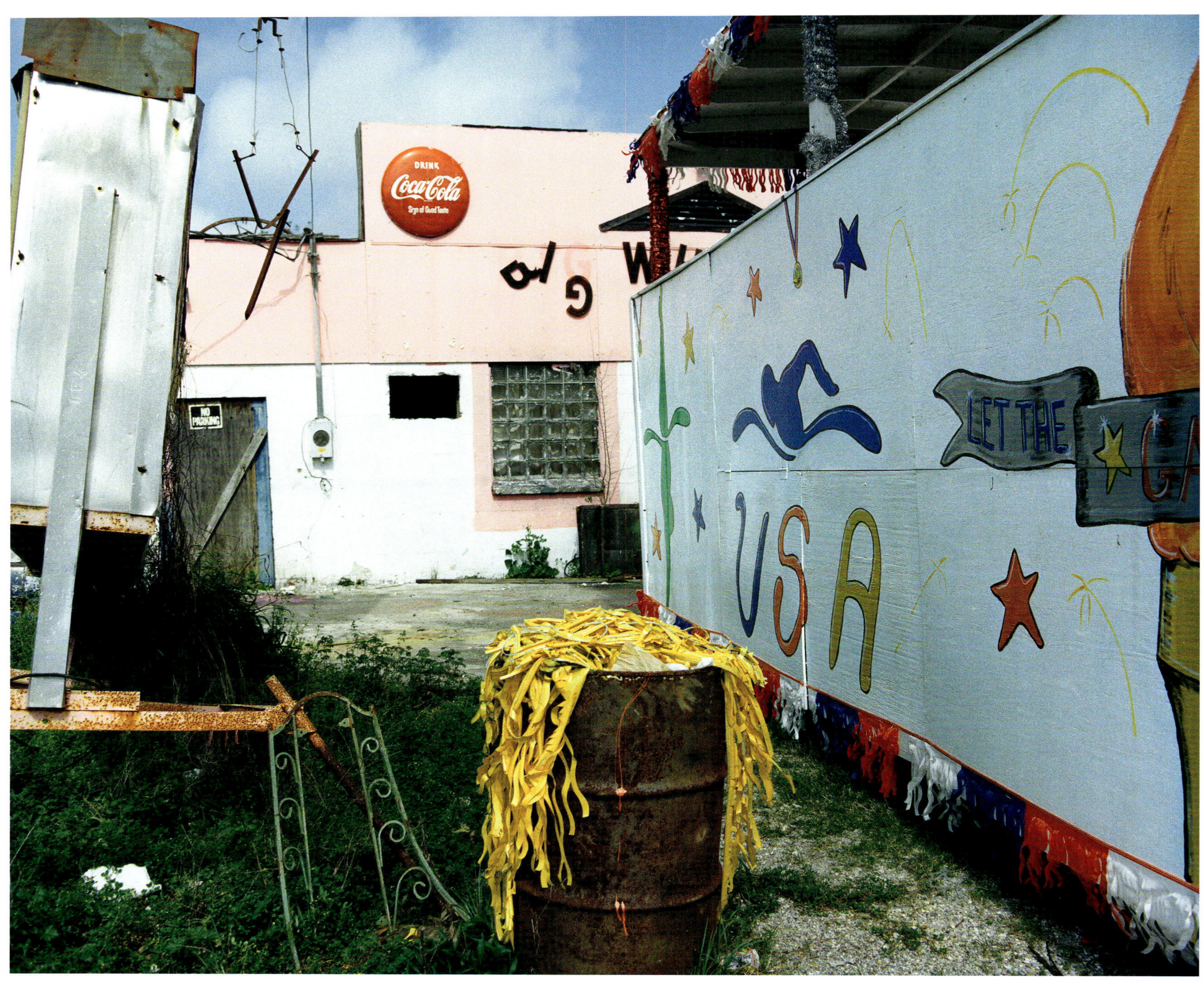
DRINK
Coca-Cola
Sign of Good Taste
NO PARKING
LET THE
USA

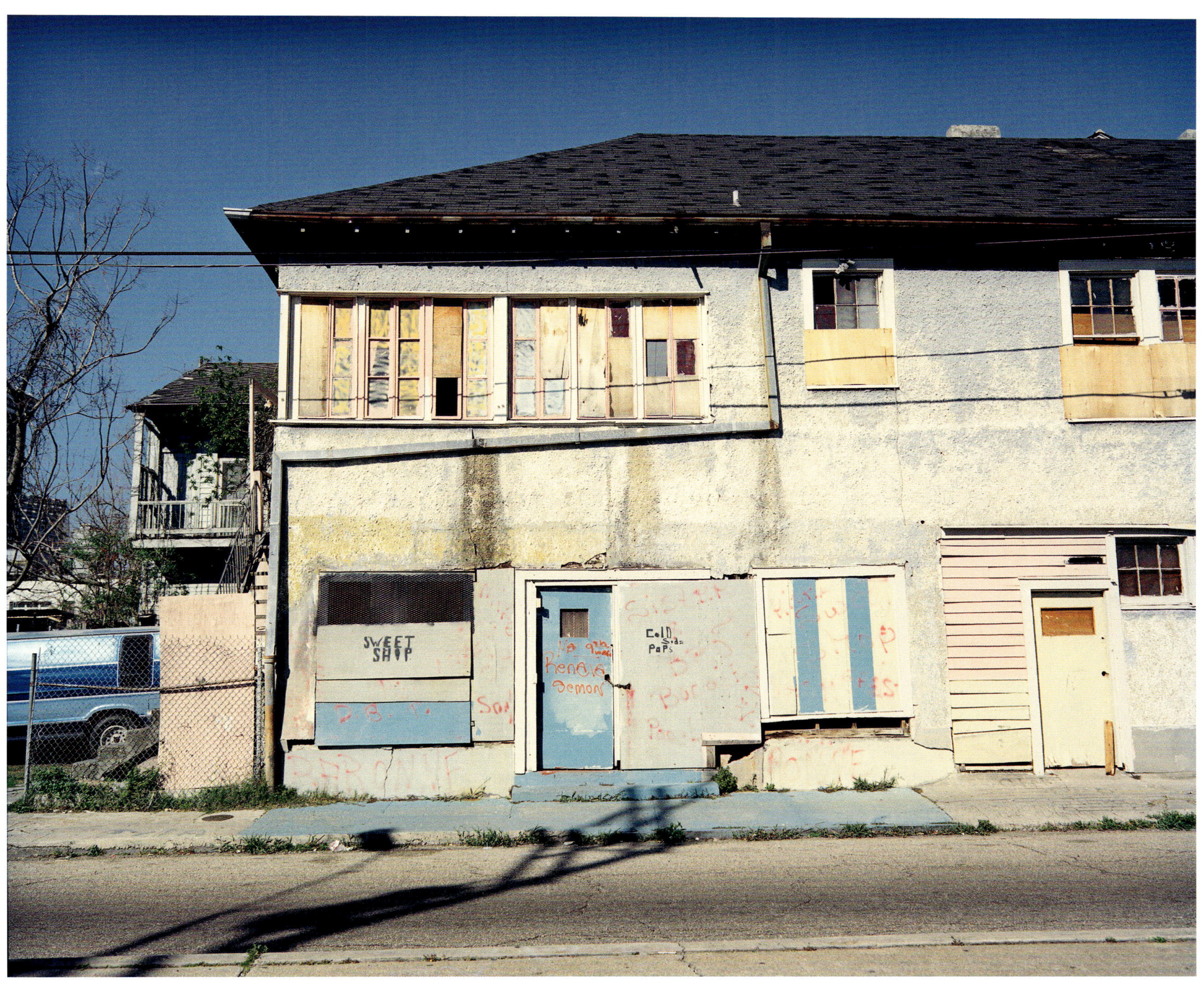
SWEET SHOP
CoLD Soda PaPs

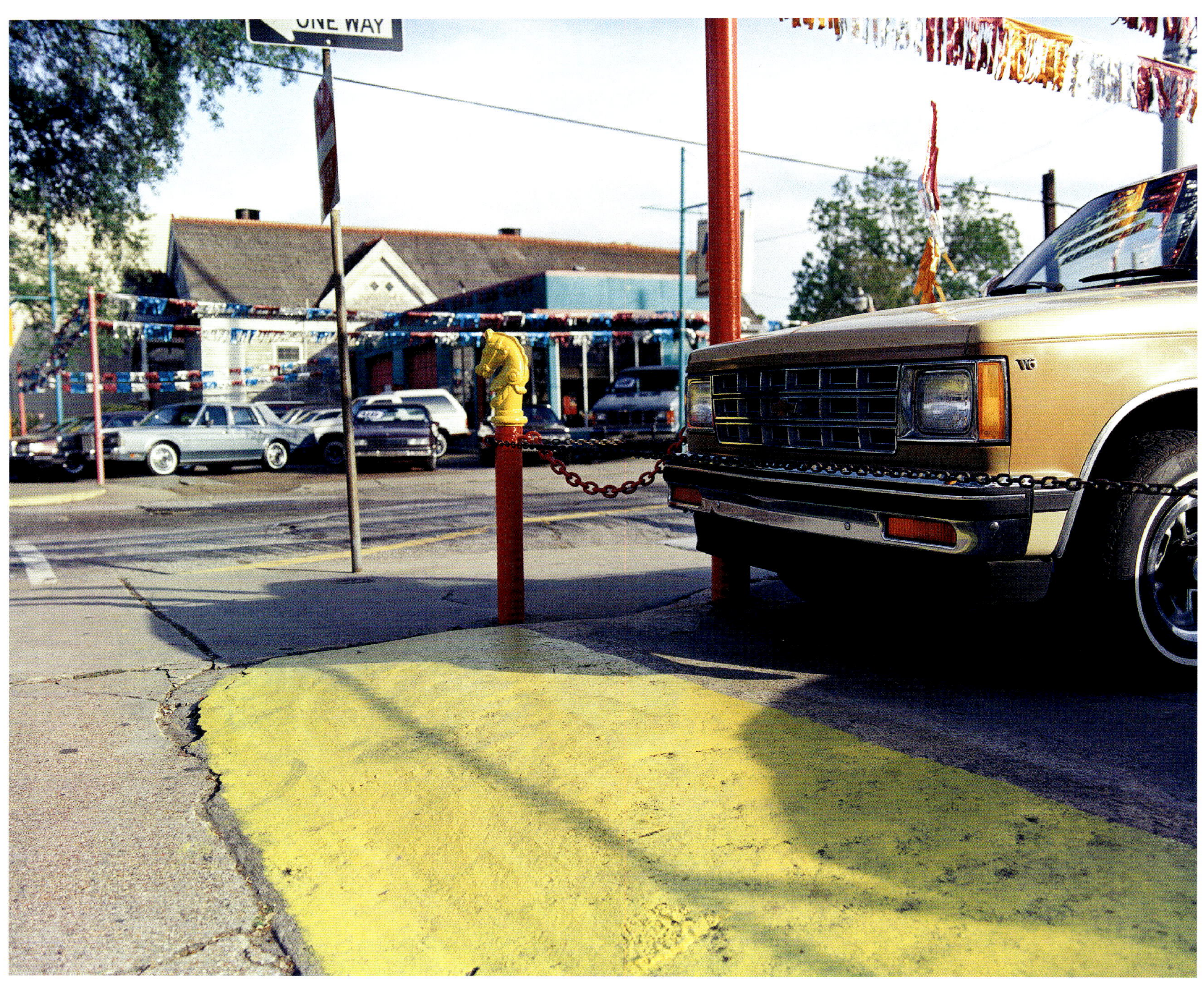
ONE WAY
V6
REDUCED

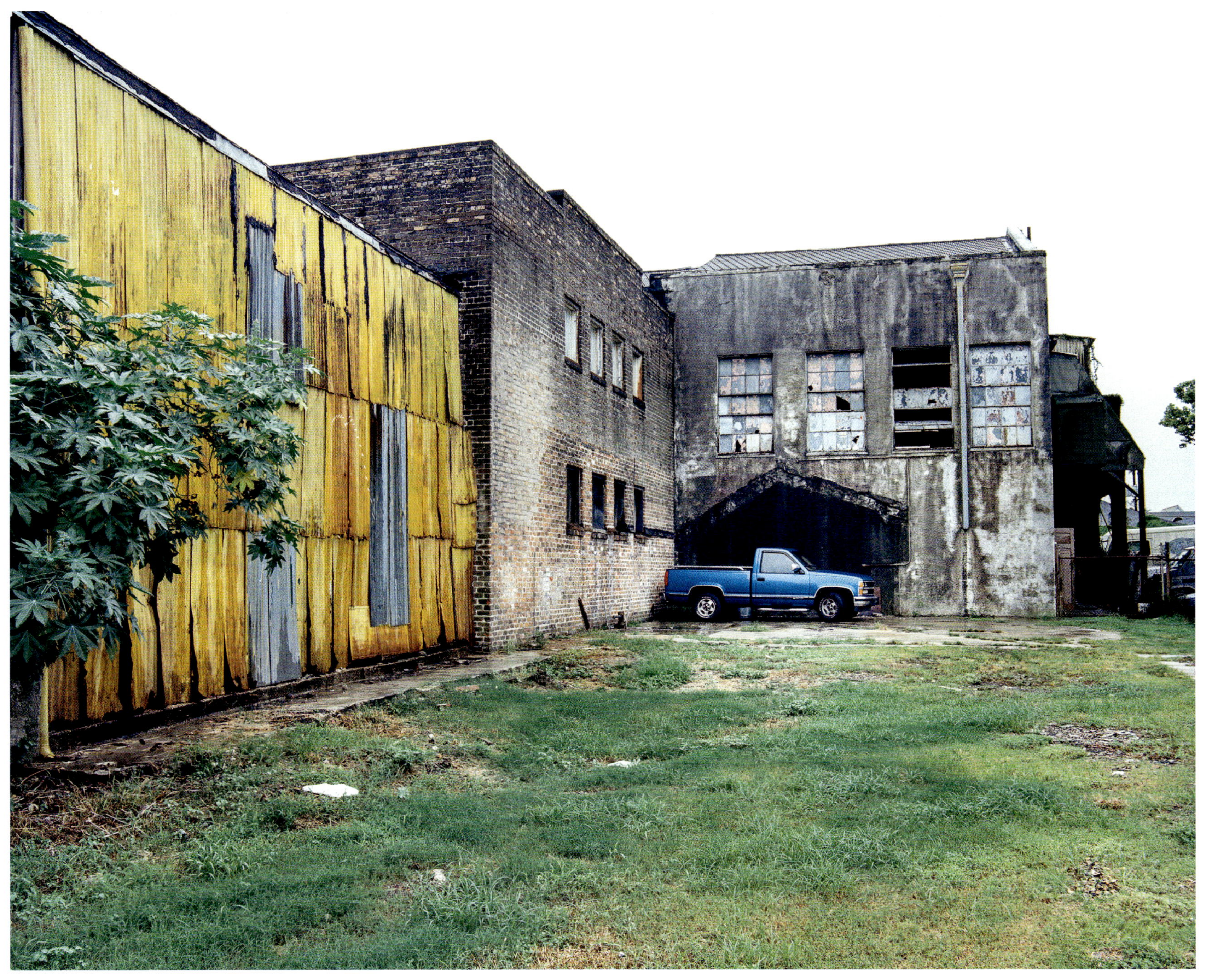

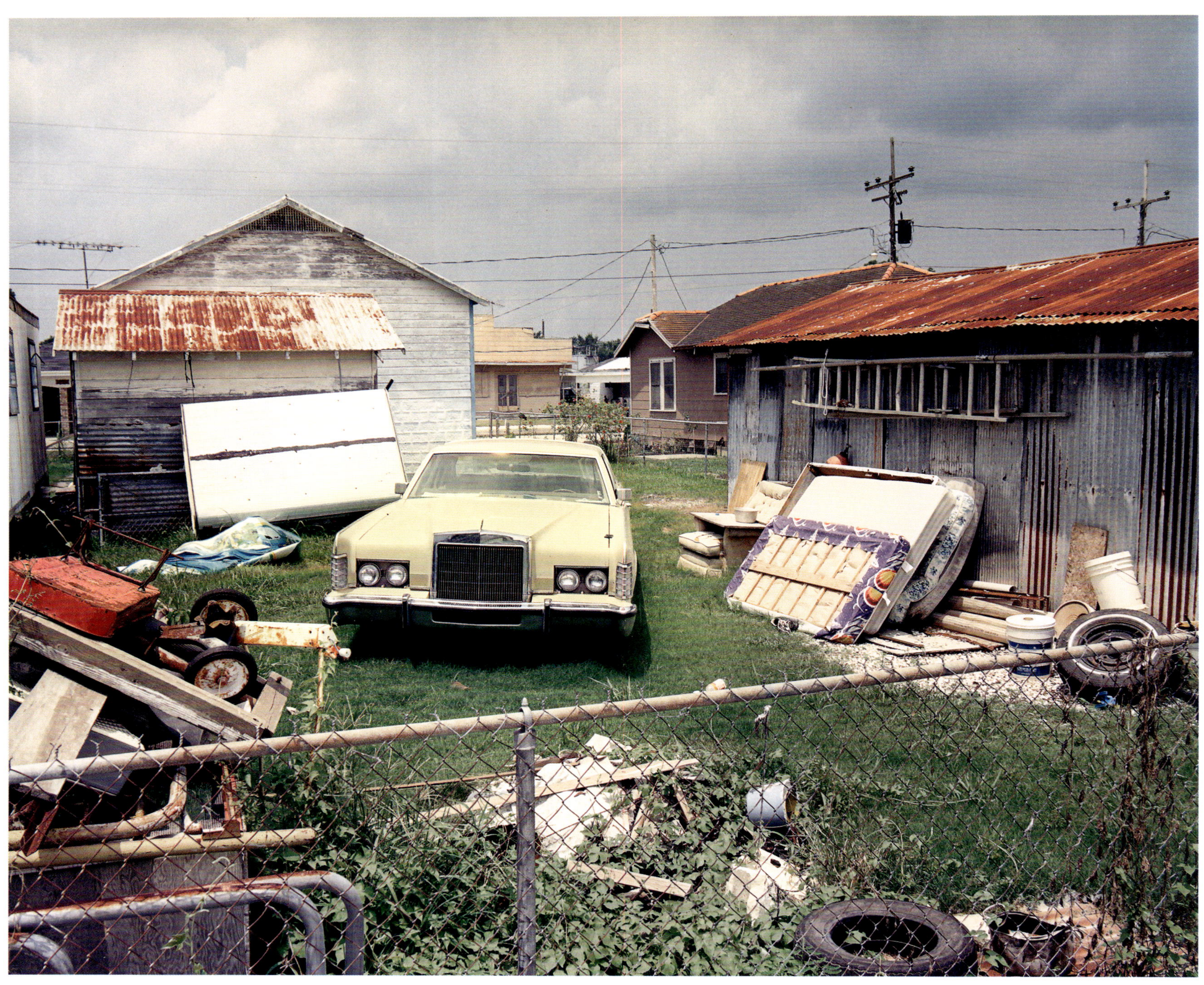

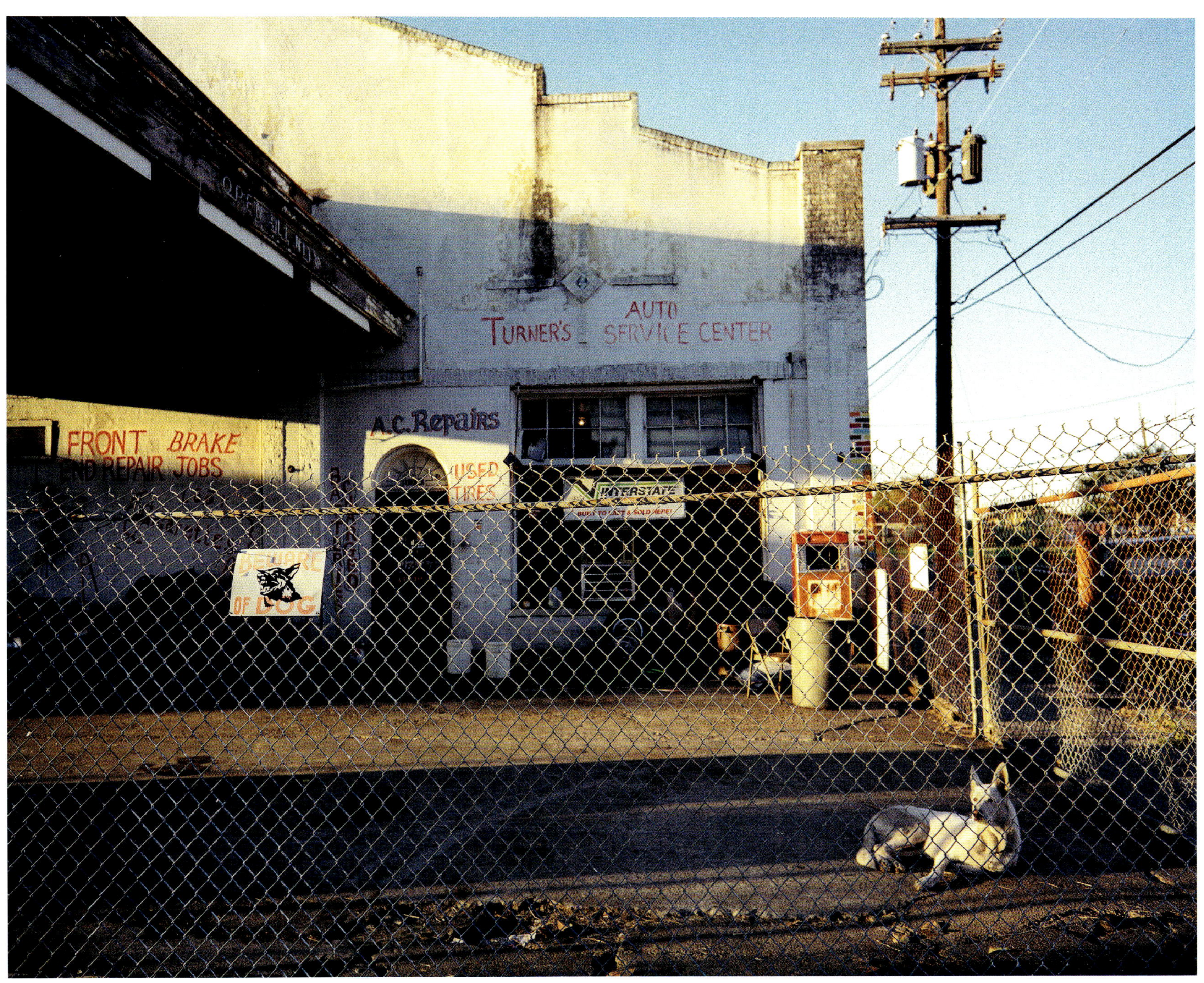
TURNER'S AUTO SERVICE CENTER
A.C. Repairs
FRONT BRAKE
END REPAIR JOBS
USED TIRES
INTERSTATE
BEWARE OF DOG

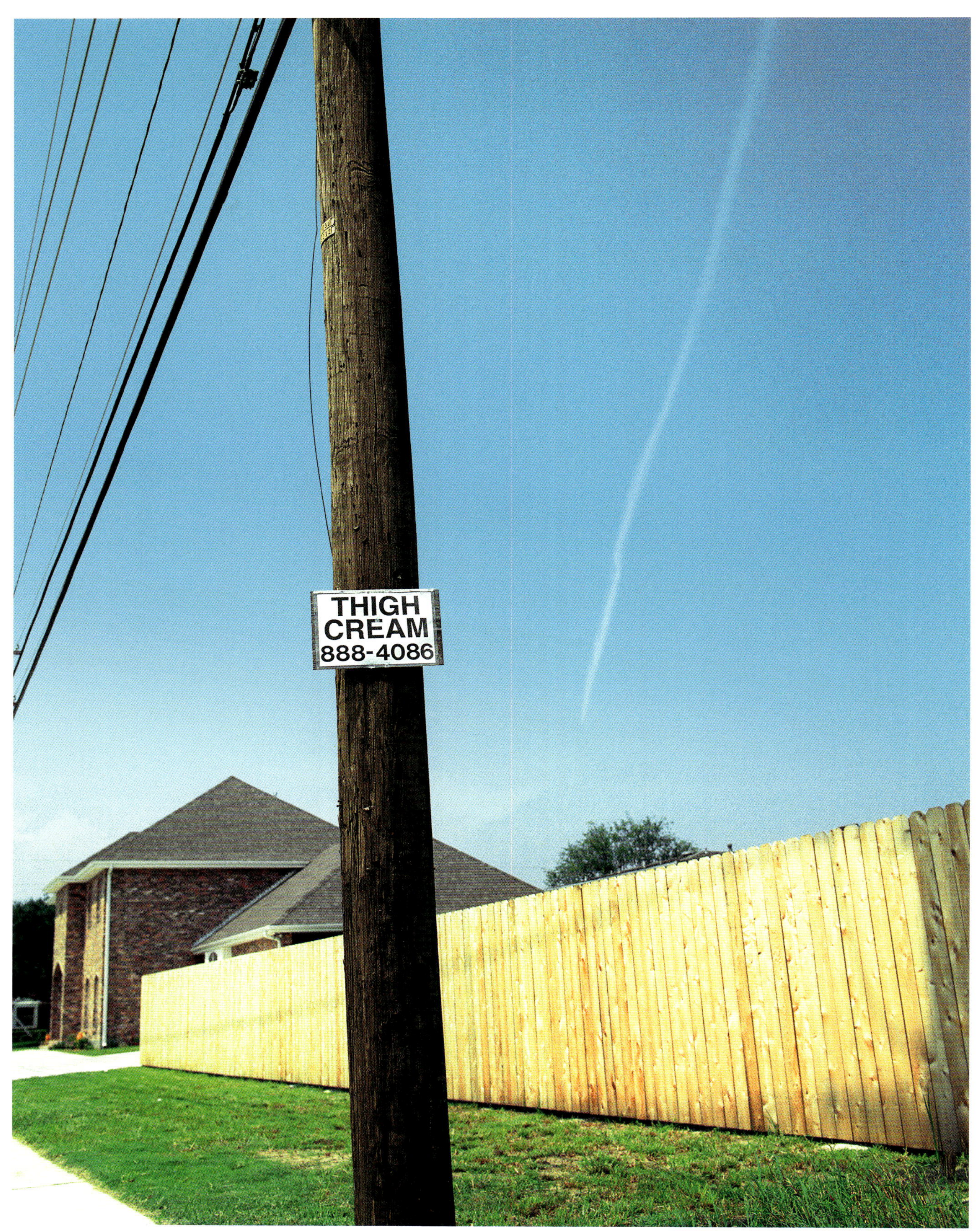
THIGH
CREAM
888-4086

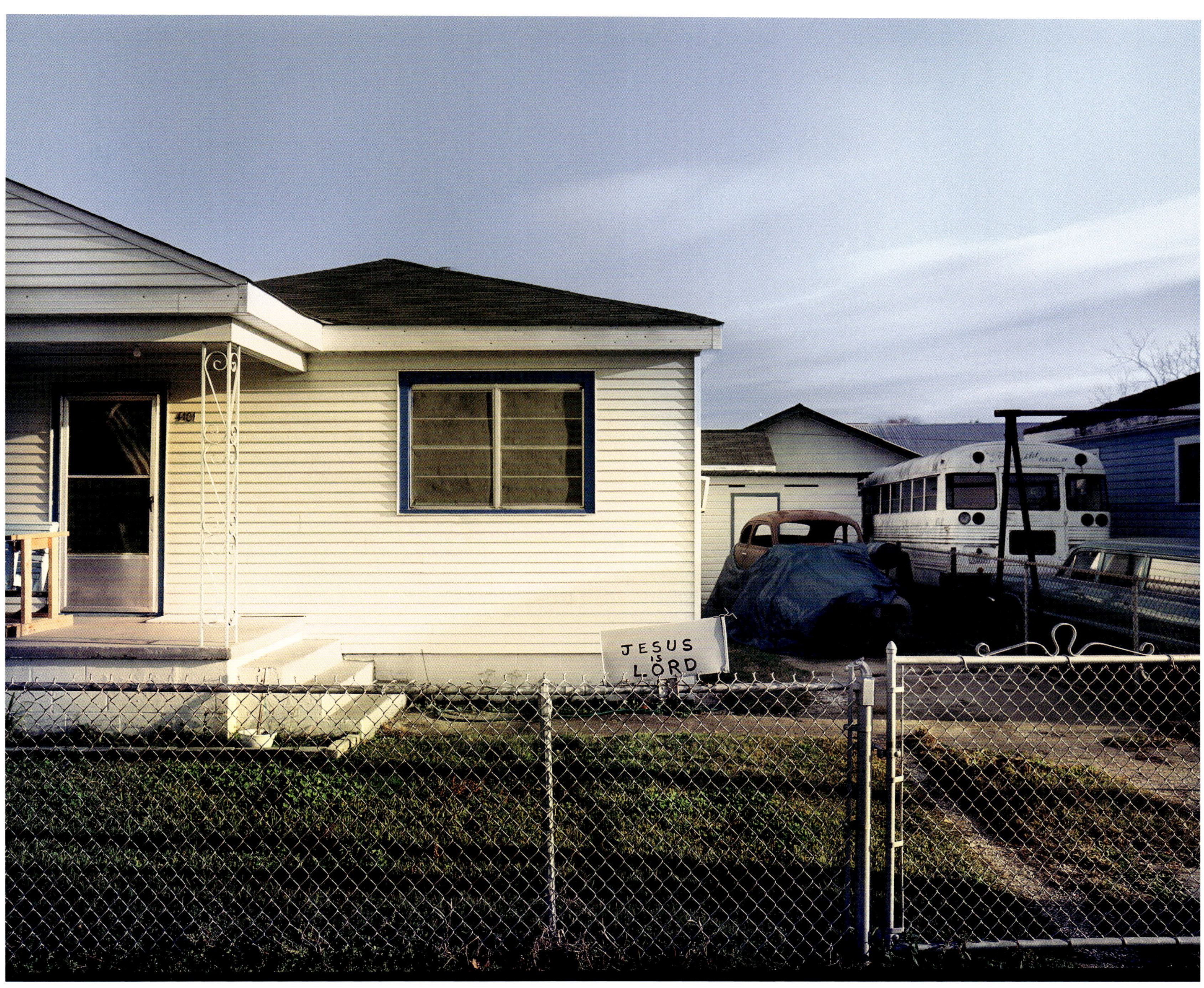
JESUS
IS
LORD

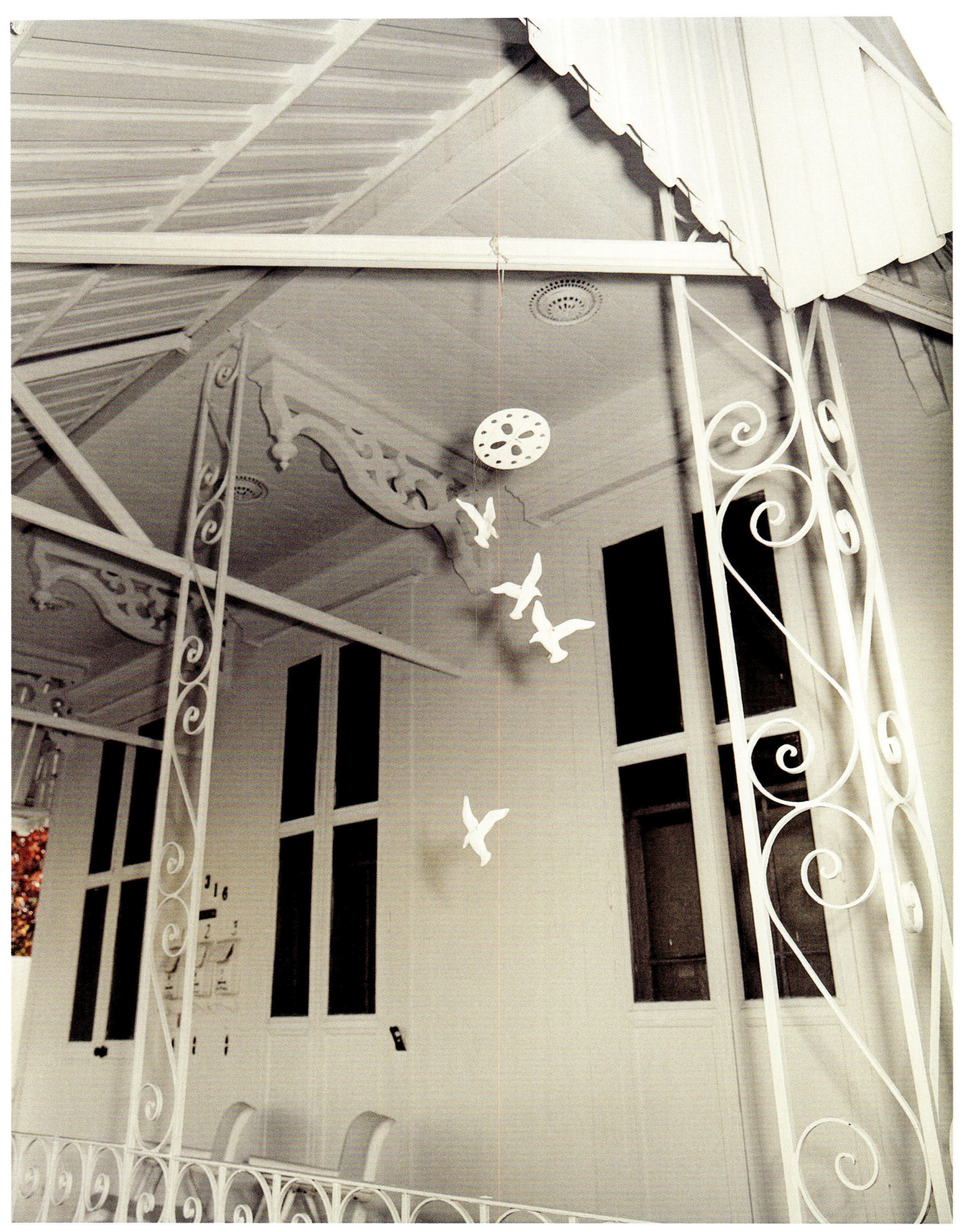
316

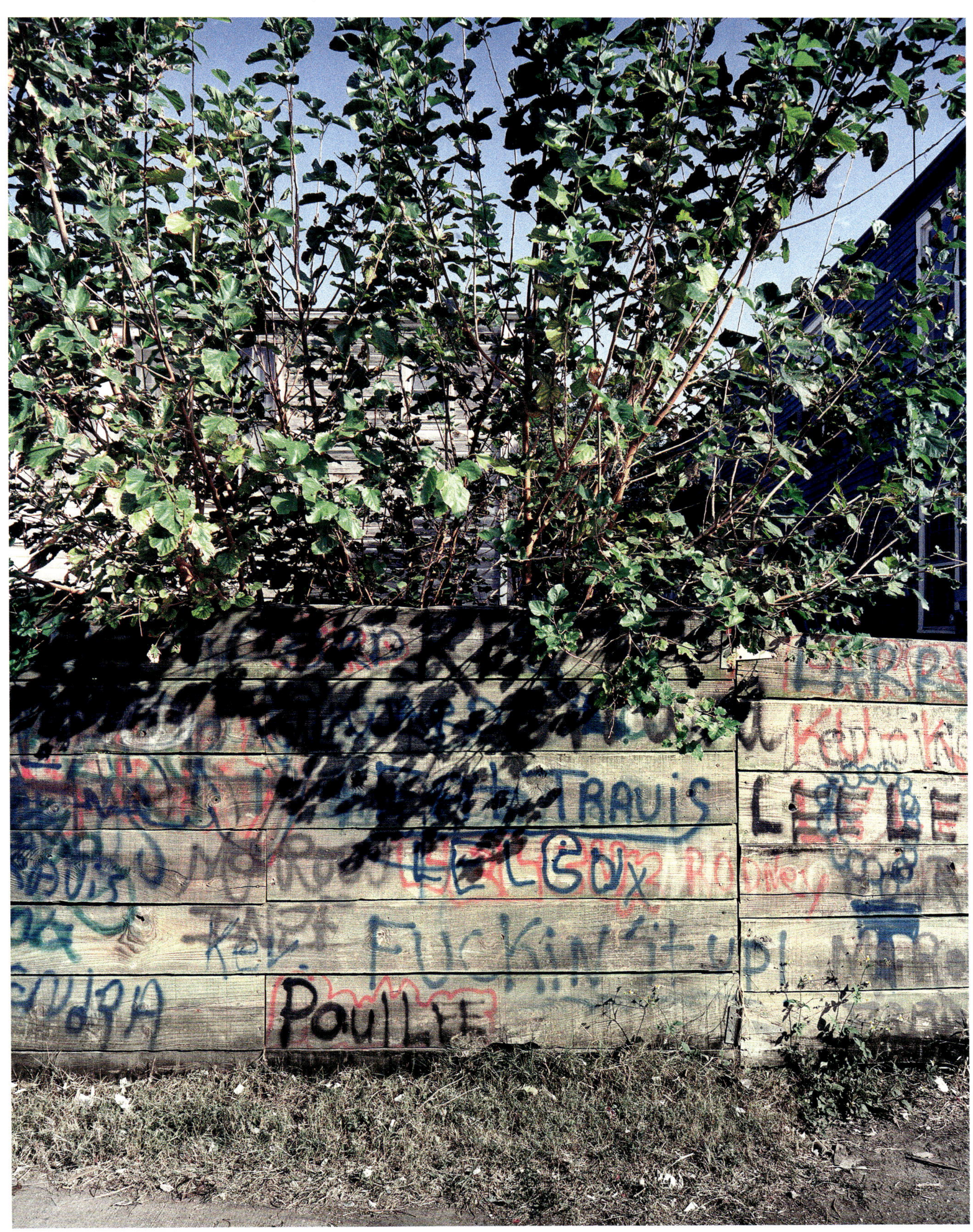

TRAVIS
LEE LEE
PaulLEE

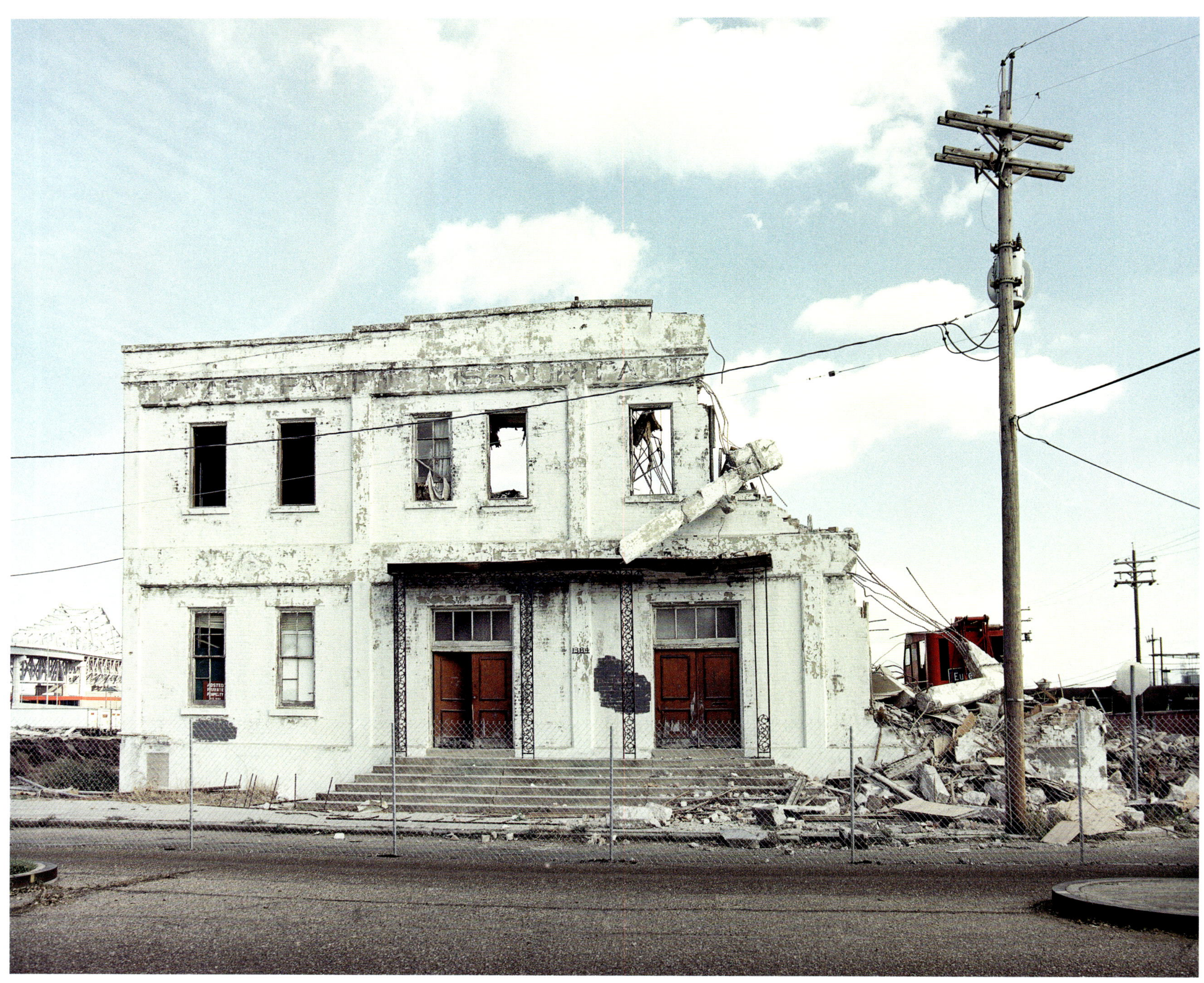

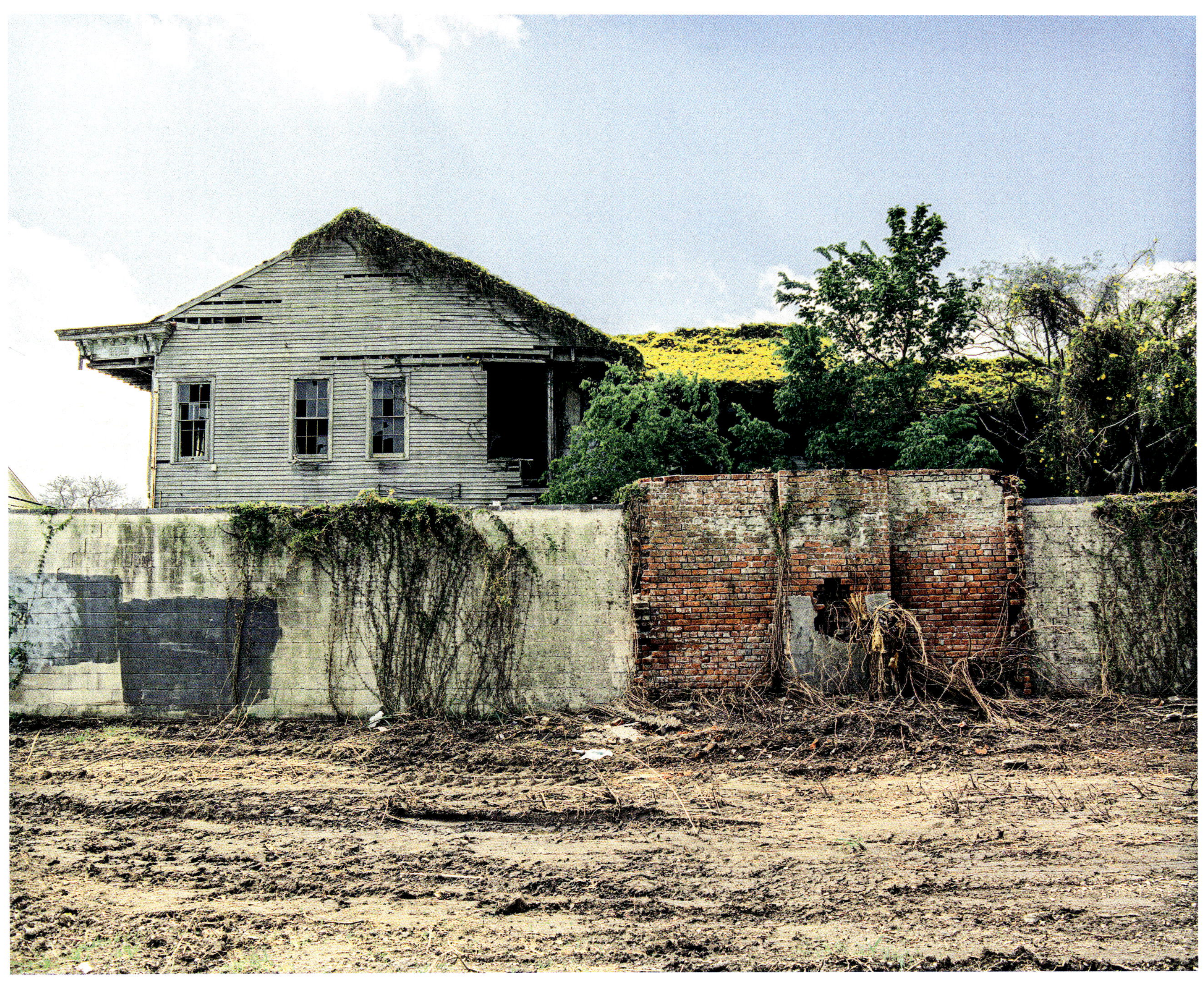

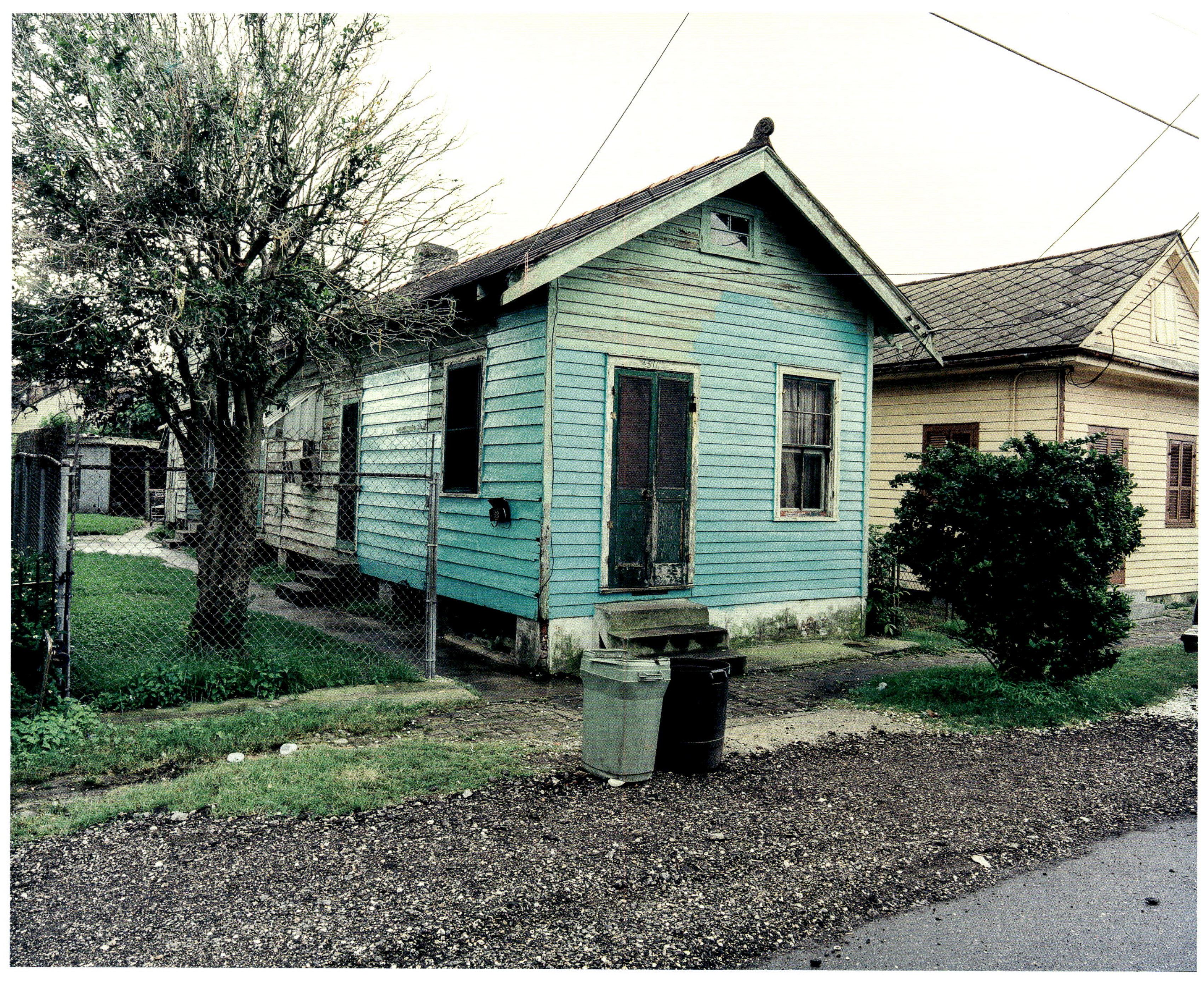

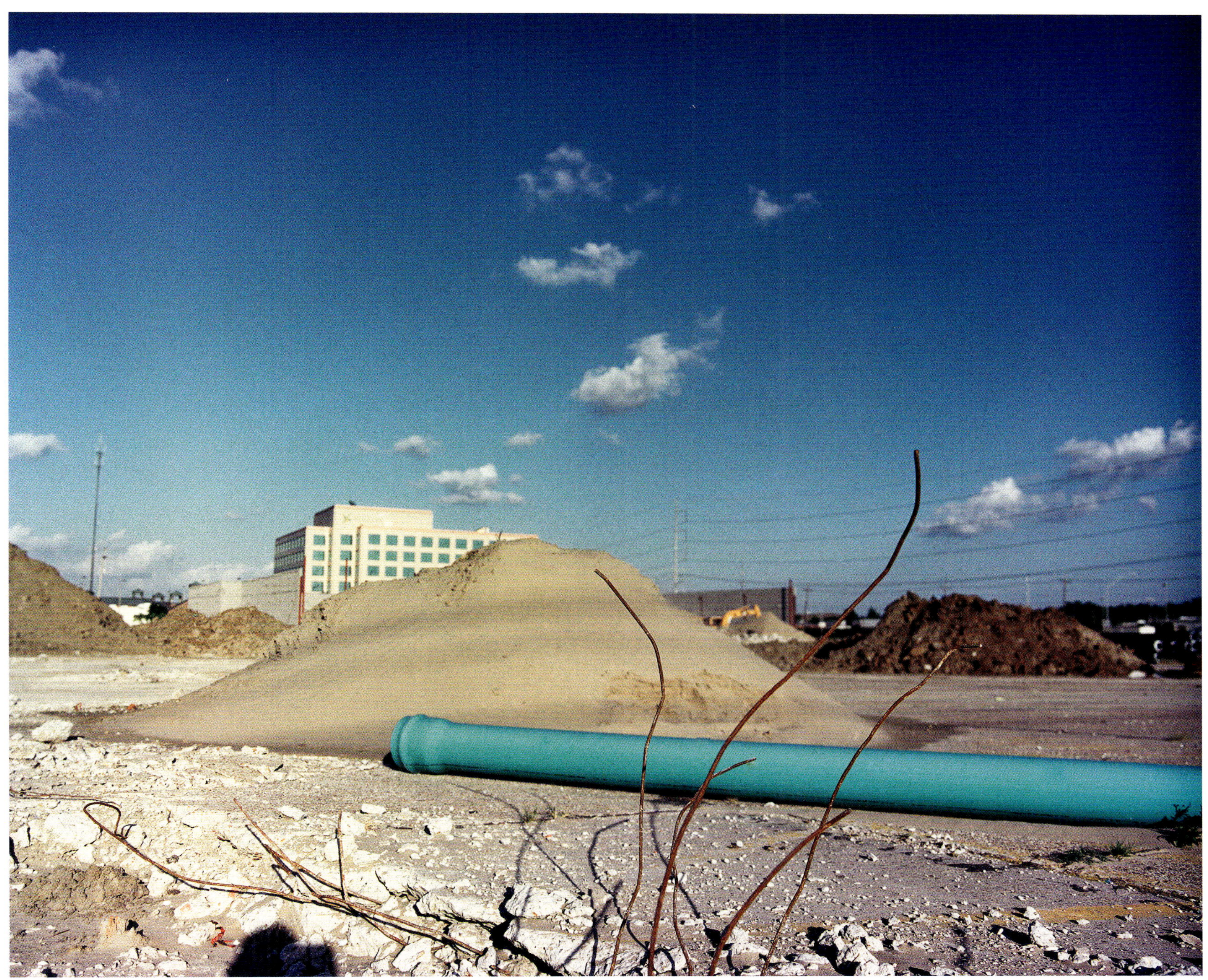

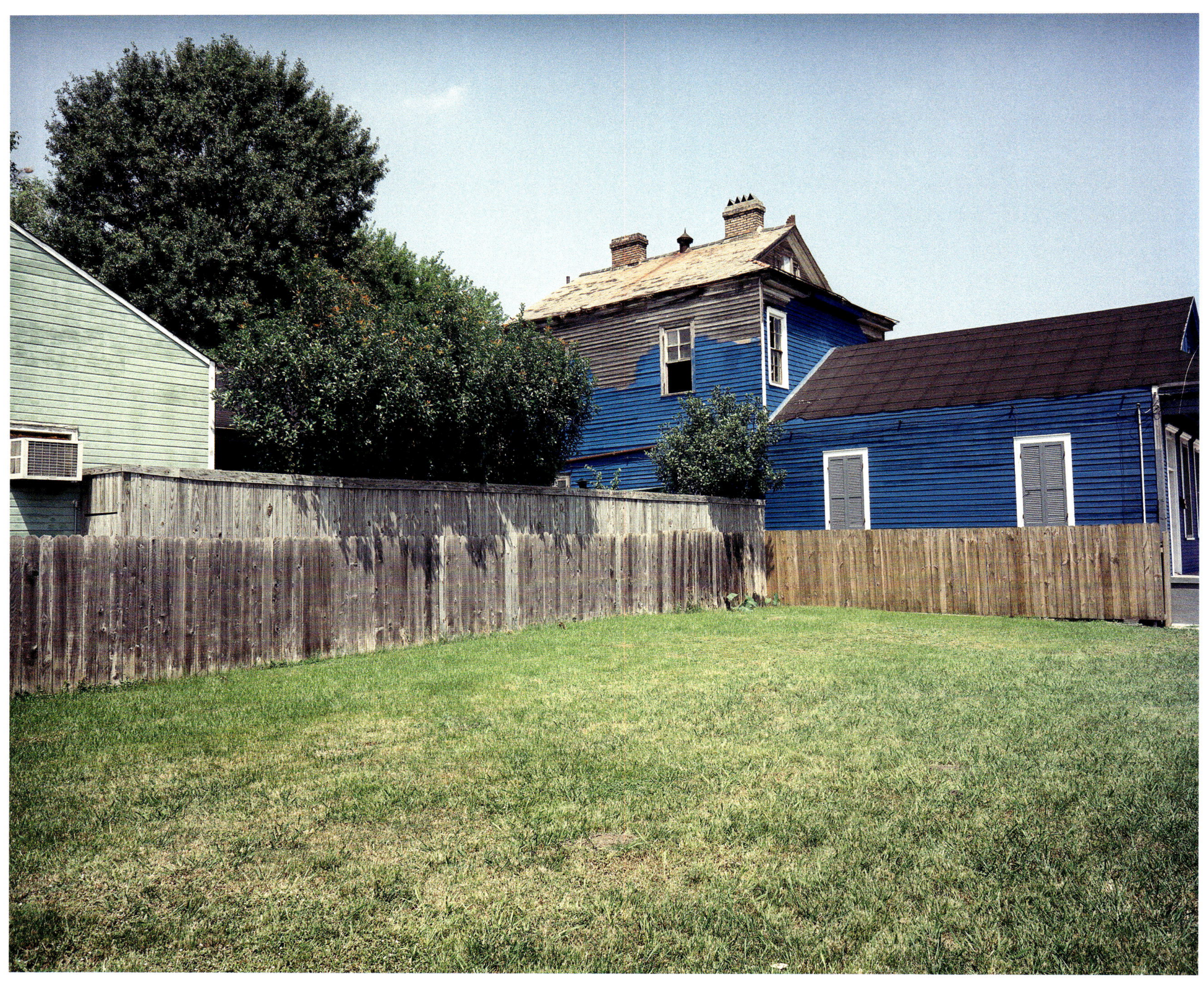

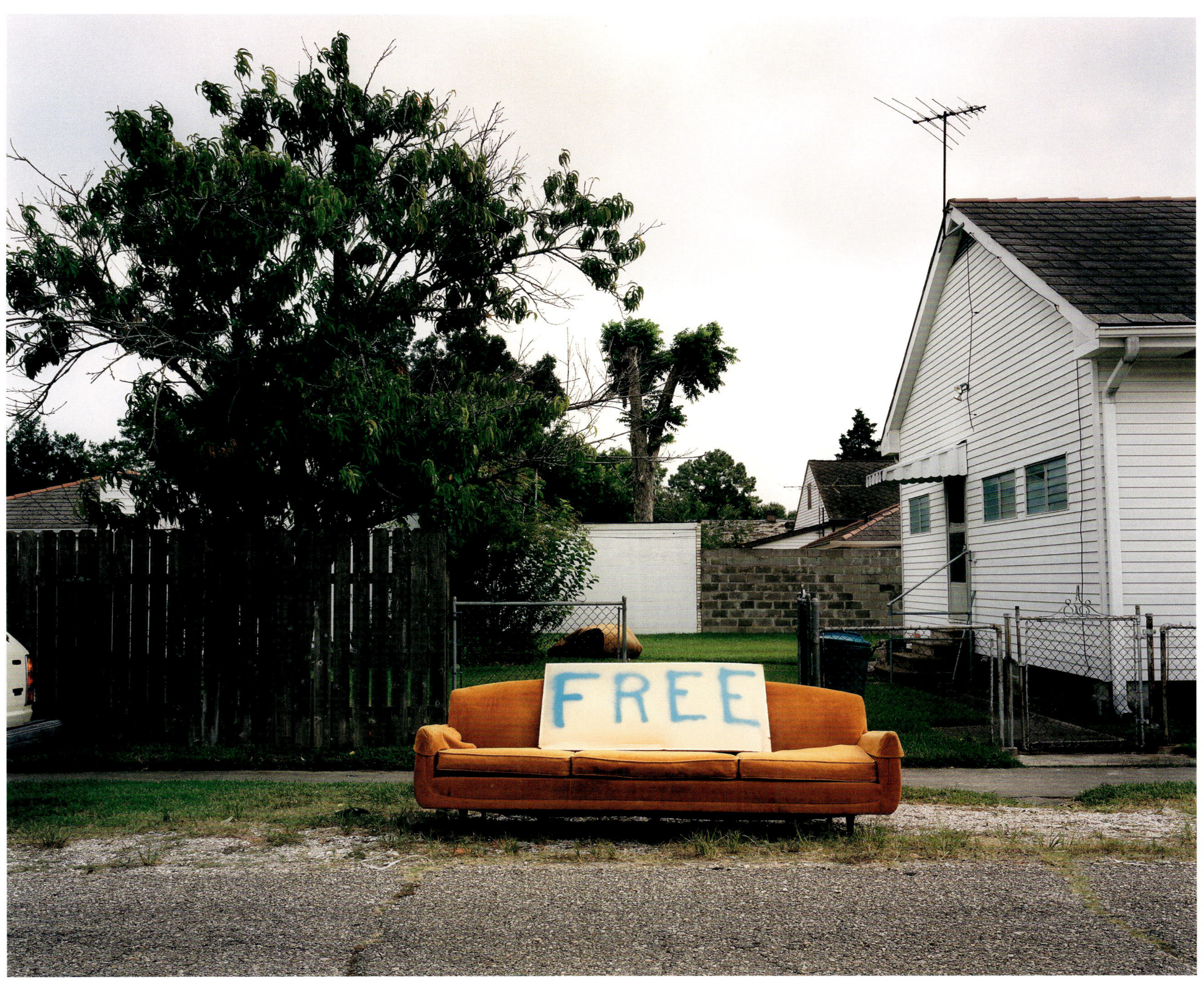
FREE

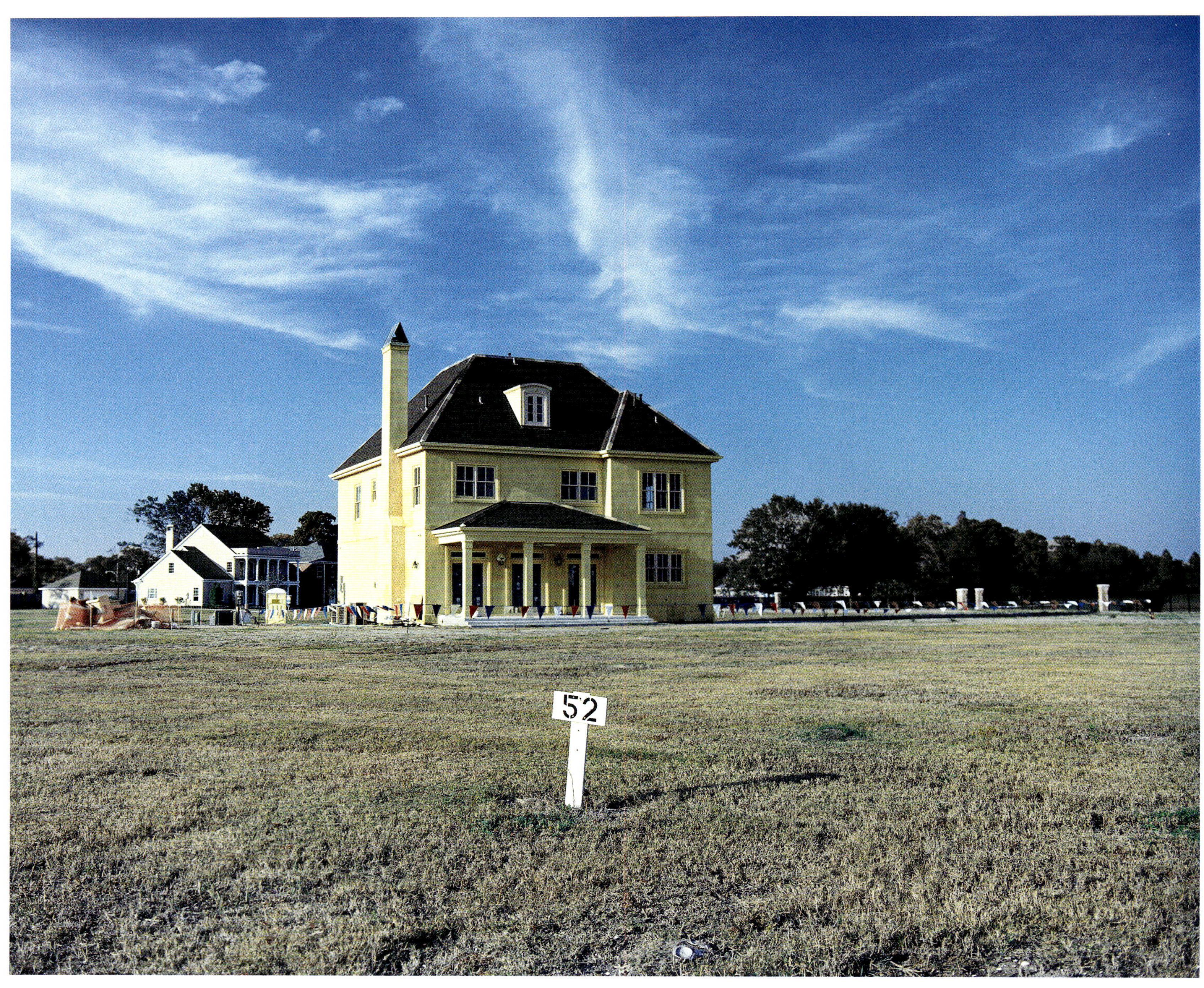
52

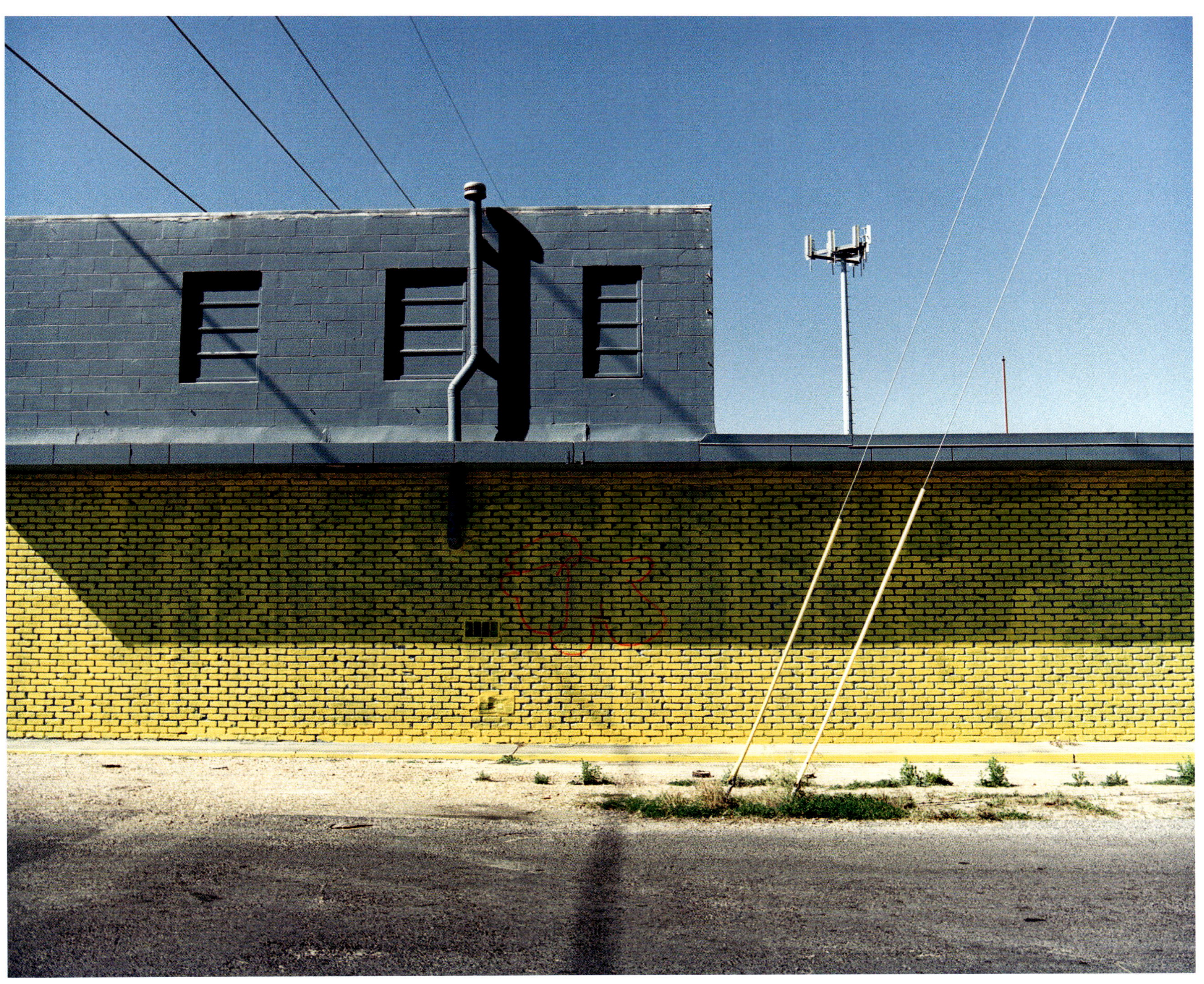

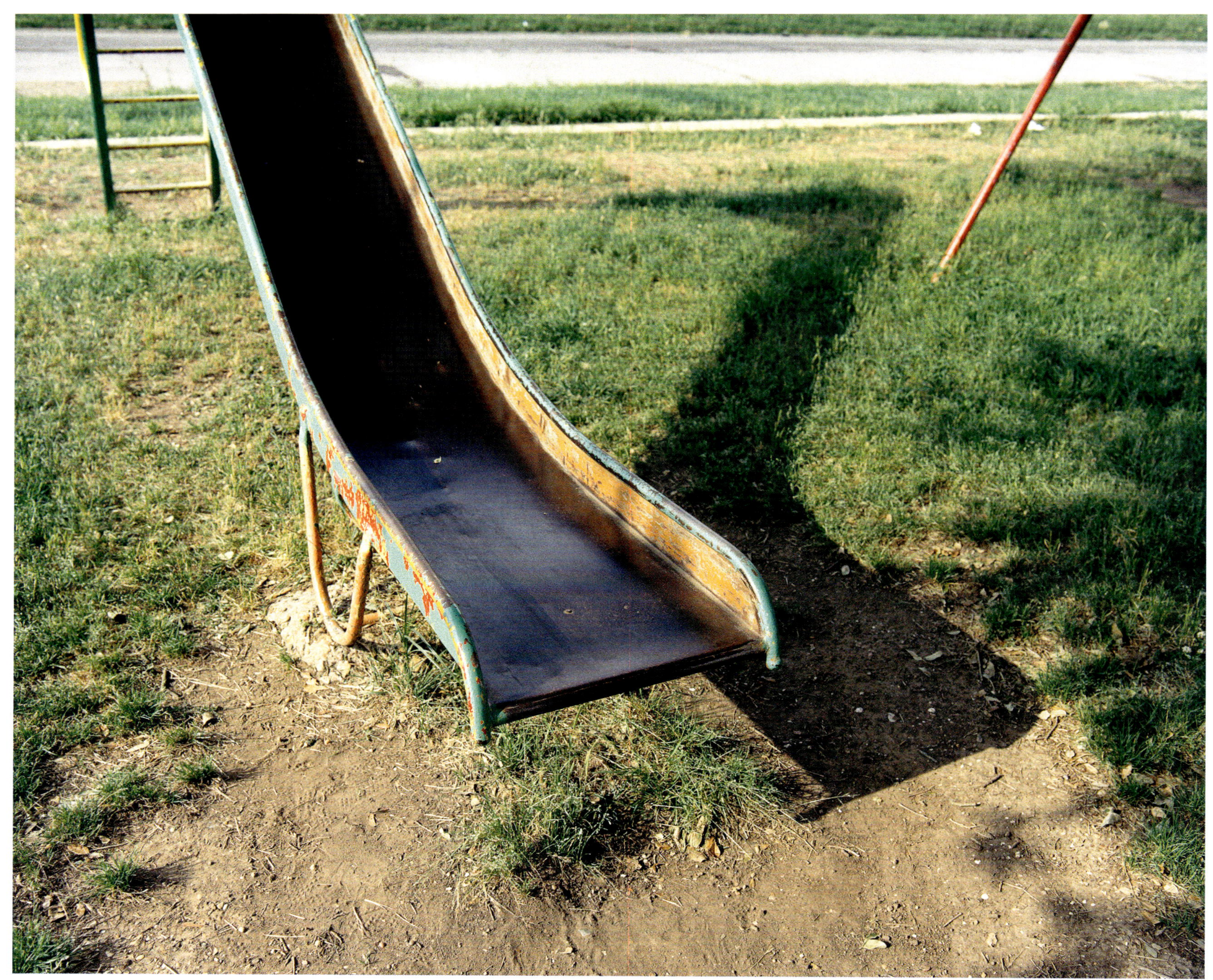

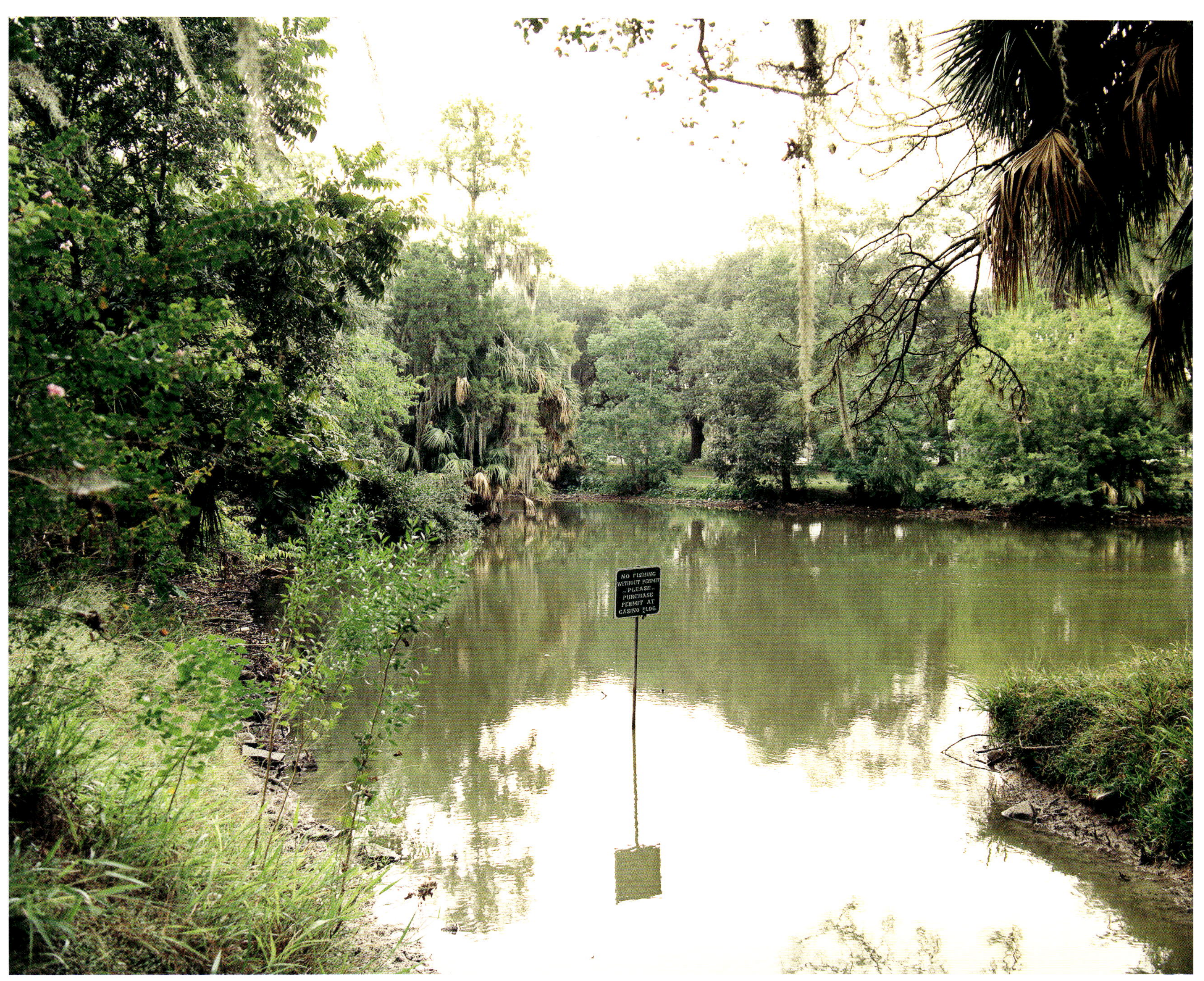
NO FISHING
WITHOUT PERMIT
PLEASE
PURCHASE
PERMIT AT
CASINO BLDG.

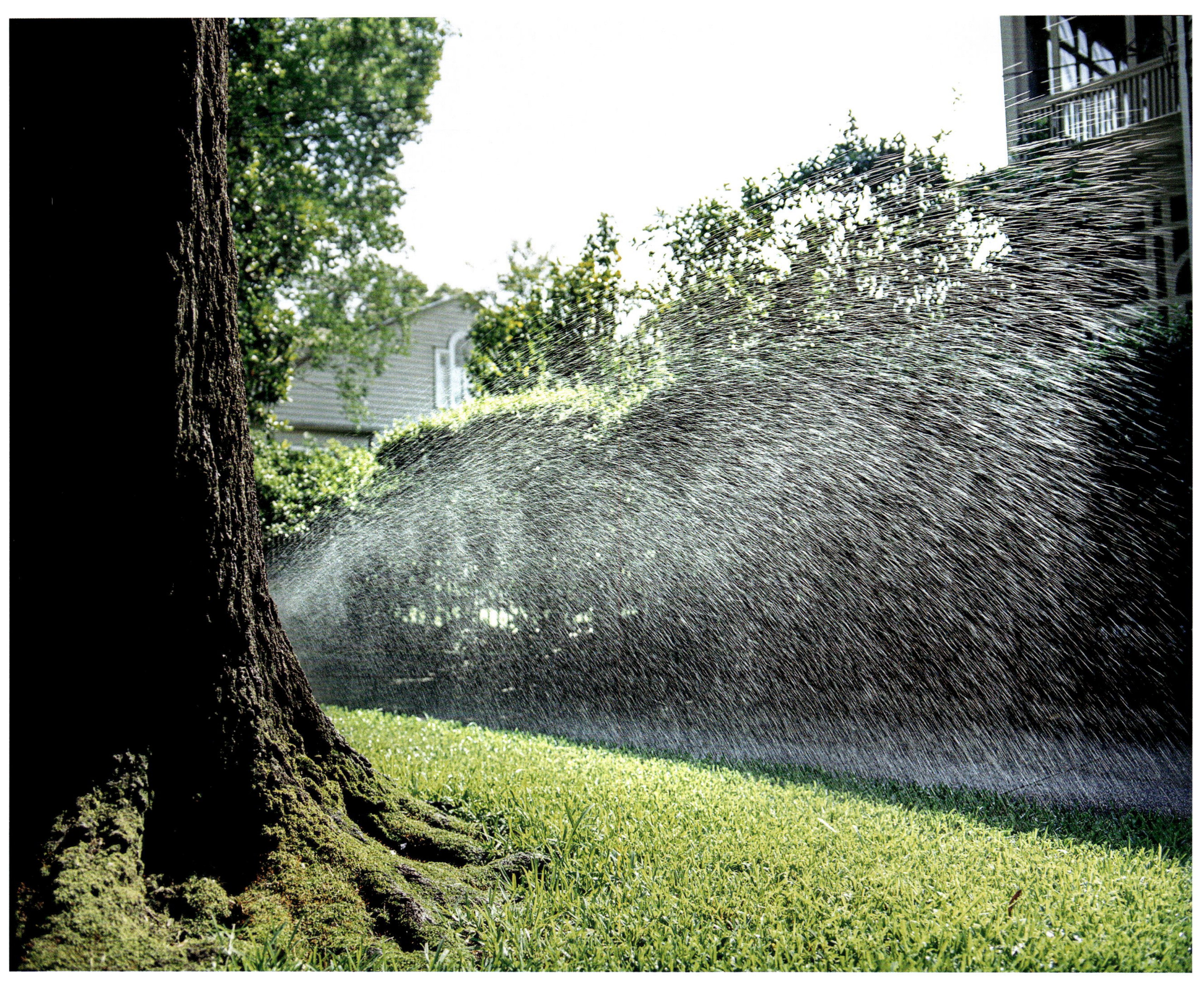

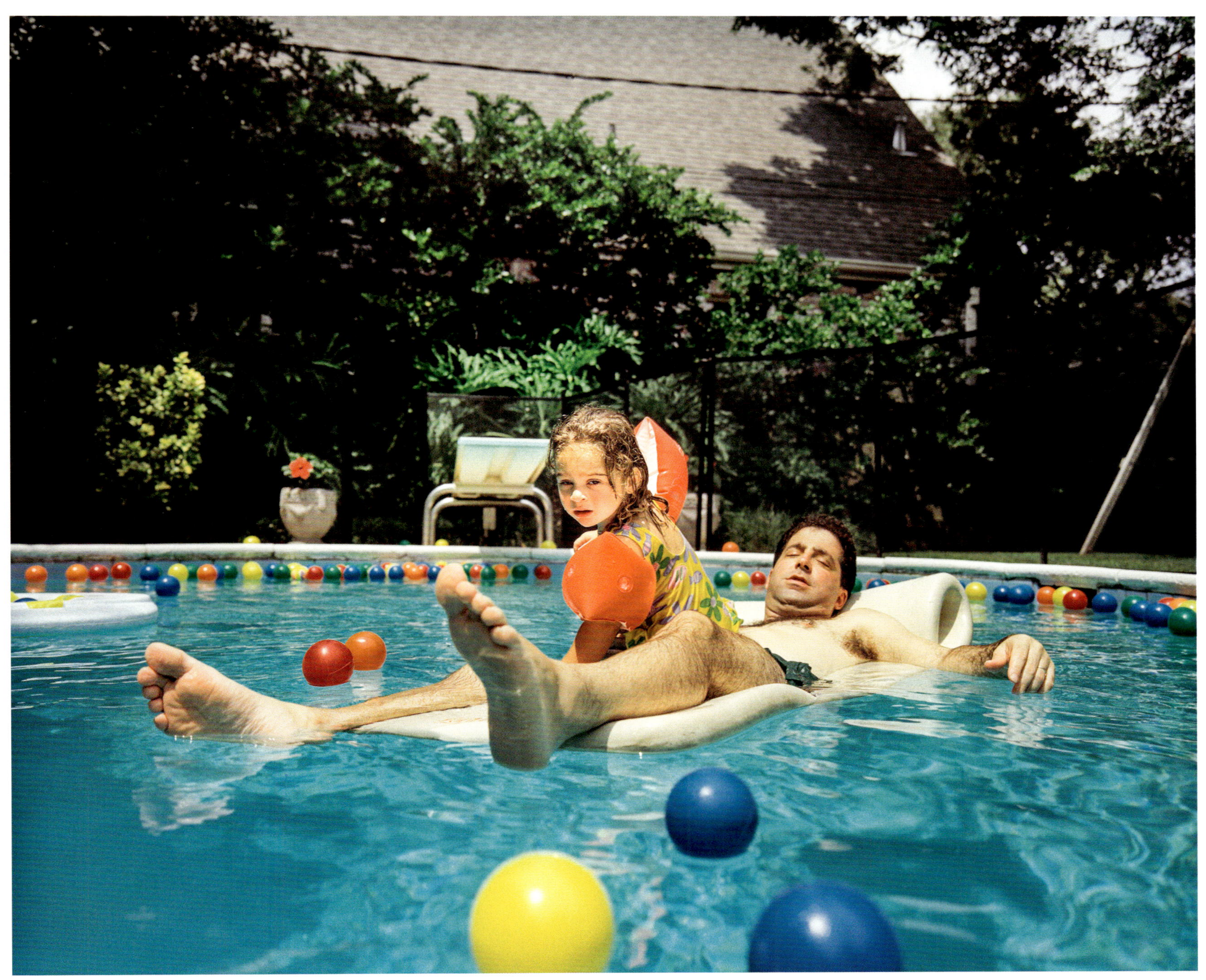

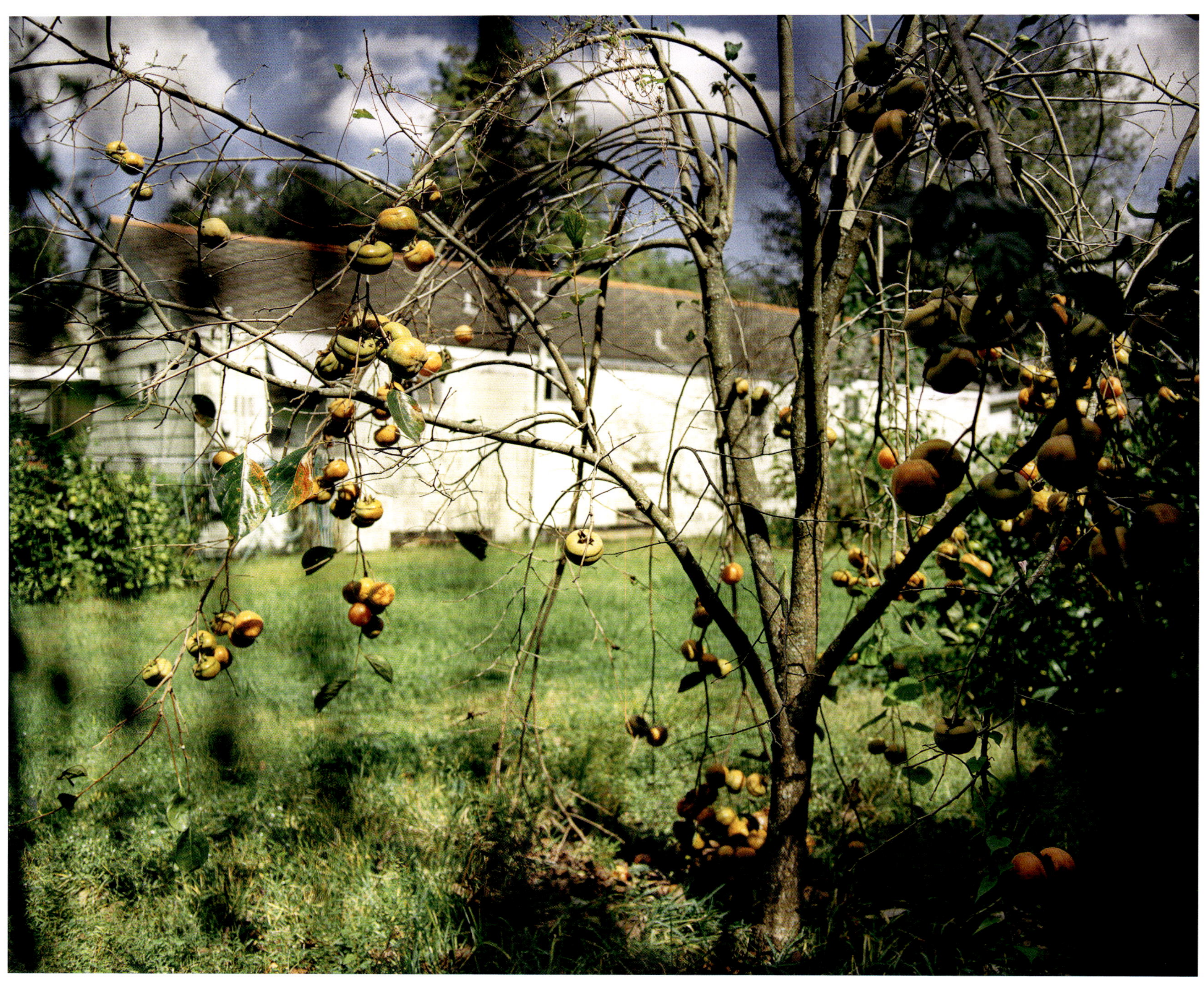

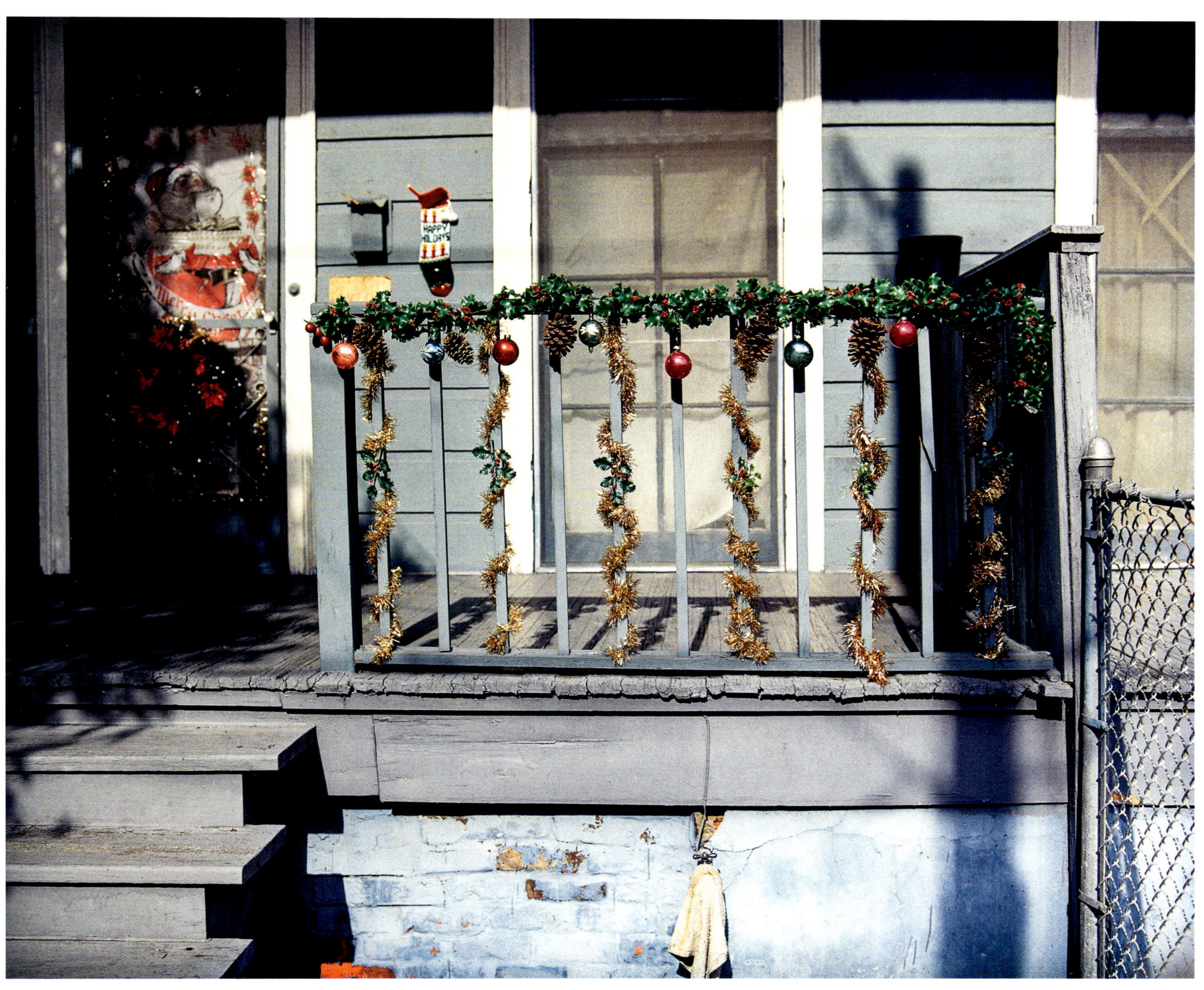
HAPPY

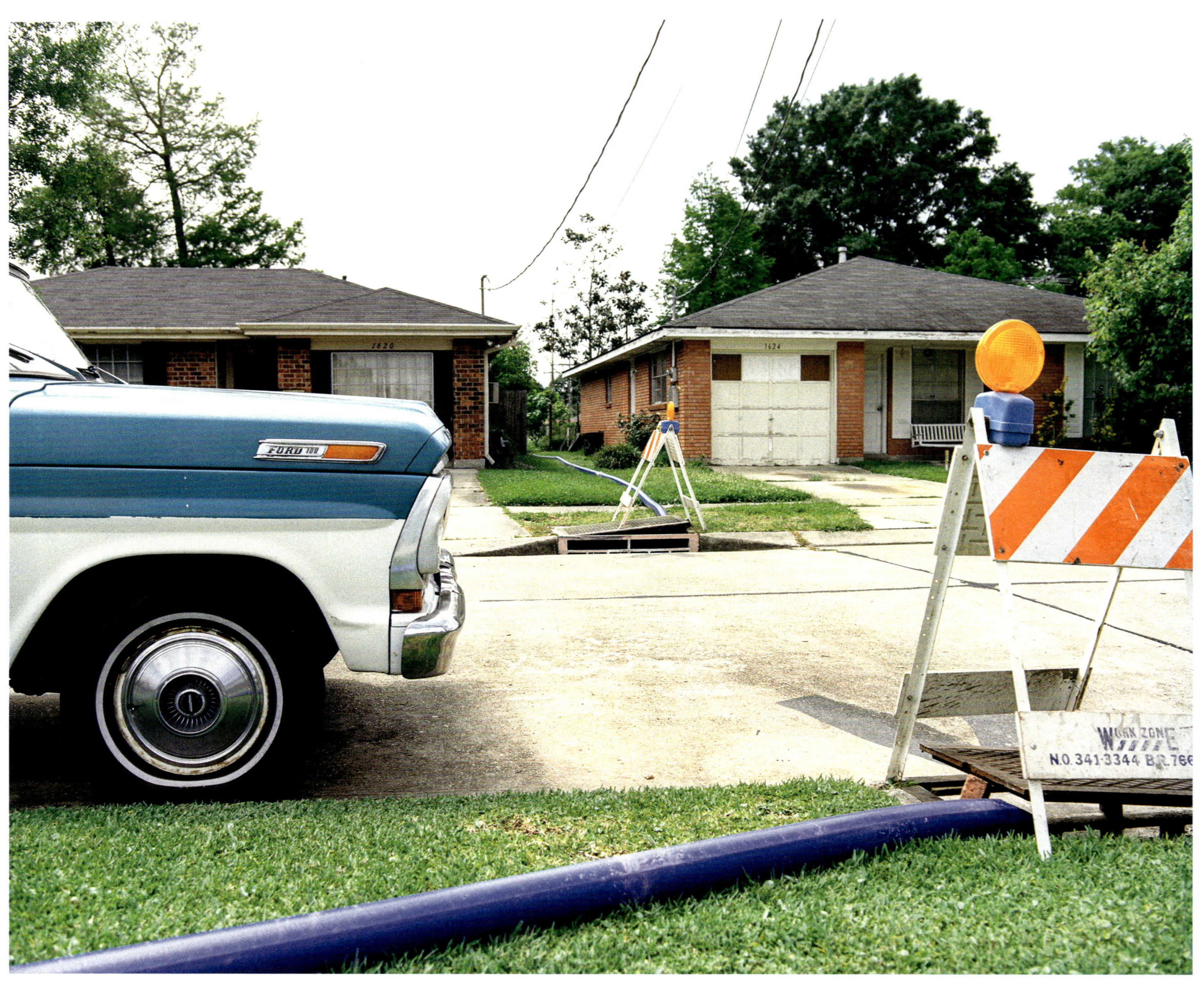
FORD
WORK ZONE
N.O. 341-3344 B.R.766

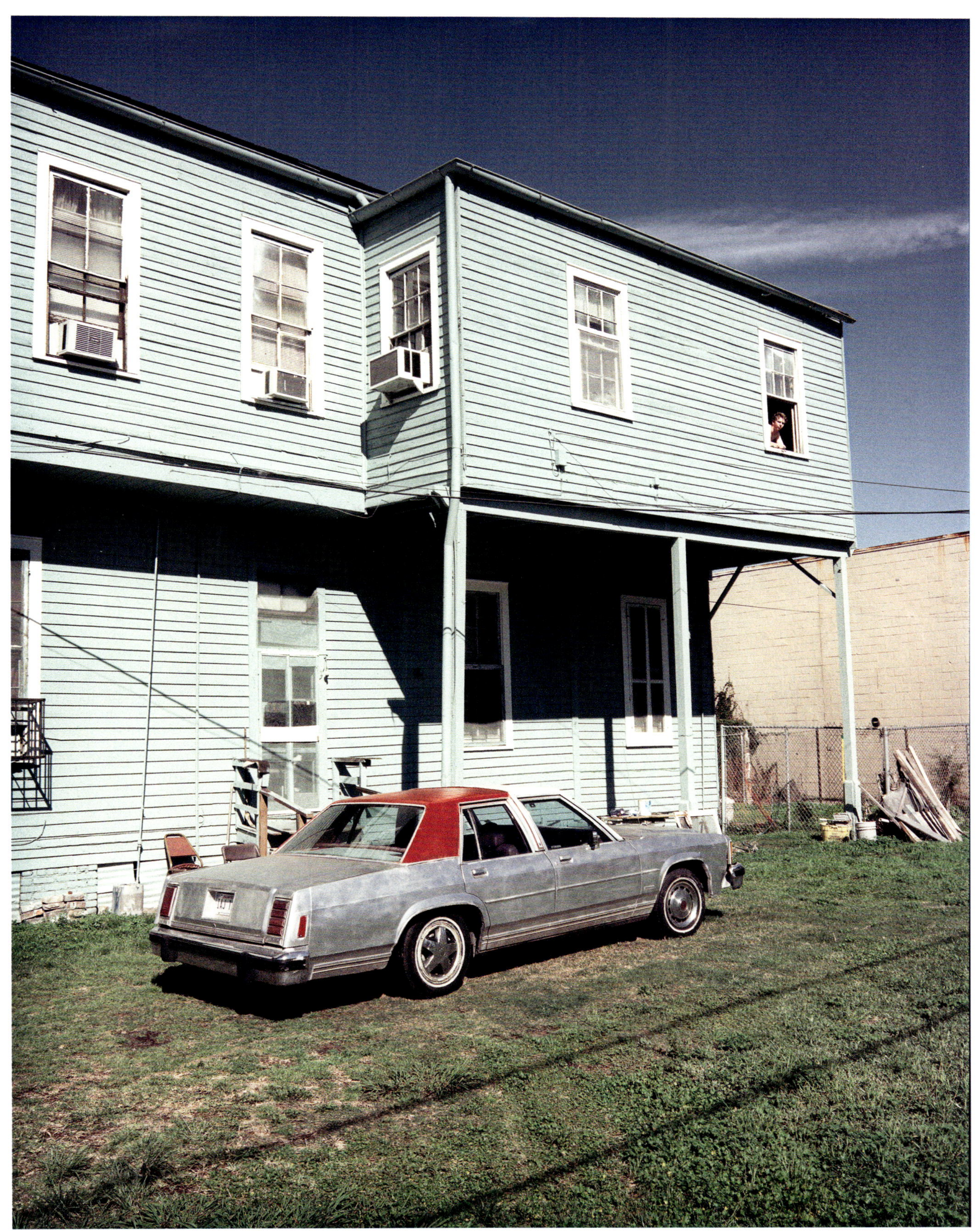

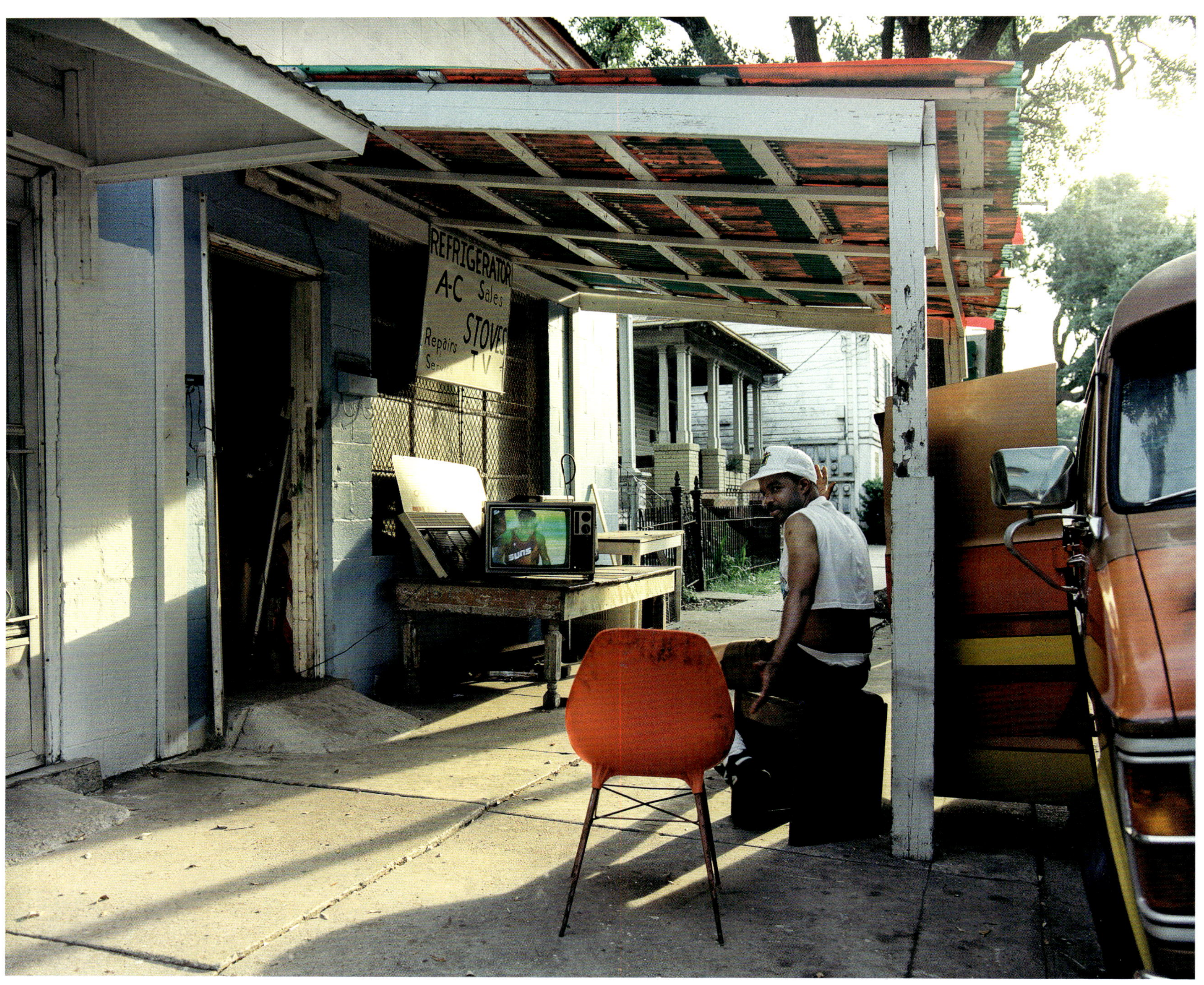
REFRIGERATOR
A-C Sales
STOVES
Repairs
Service
TV
SUNS

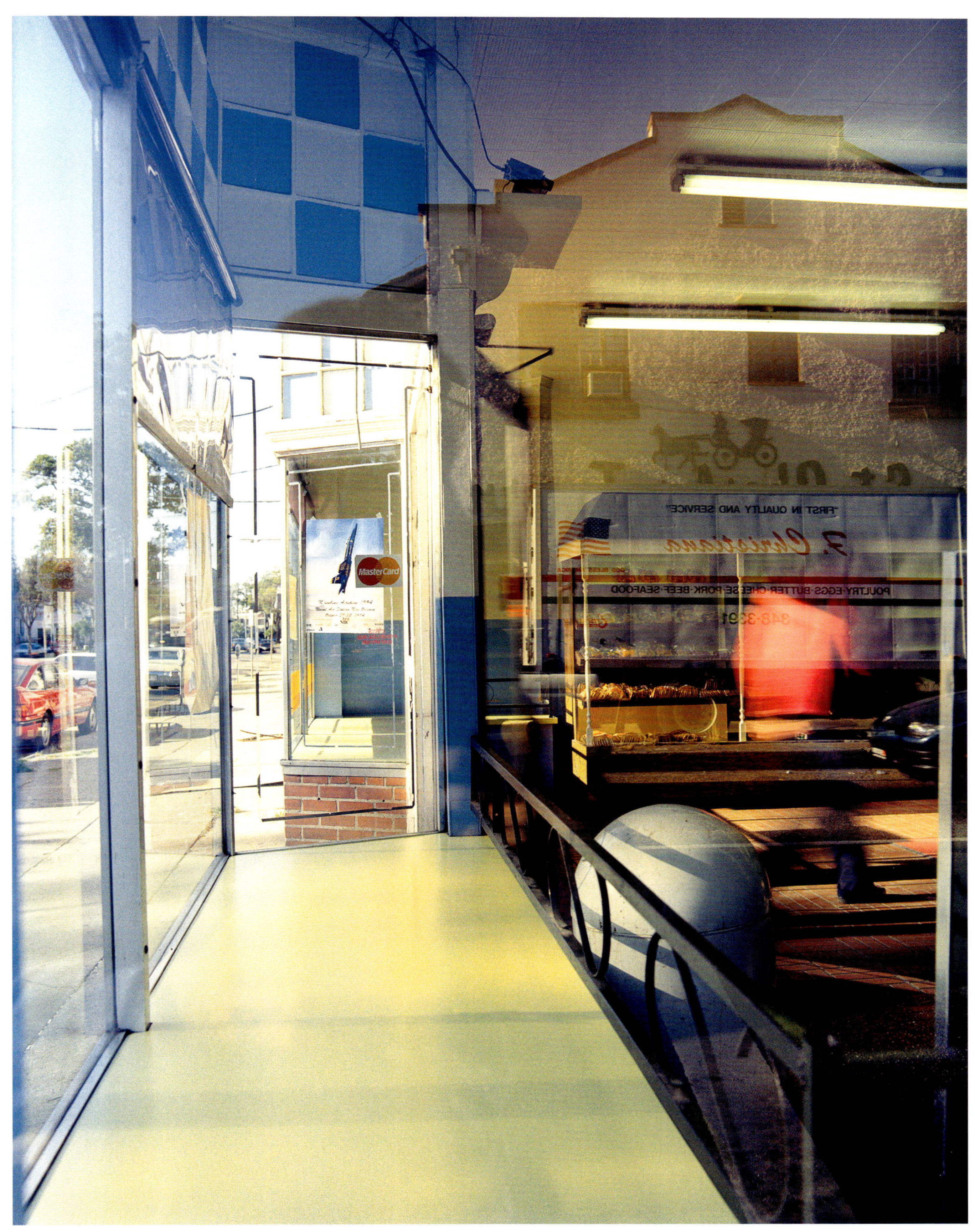

MasterCard
"FIRST IN QUALITY AND SERVICE"
POULTRY·EGGS·BUTTER·CHEESE·PORK·BEEF·SEAFOOD

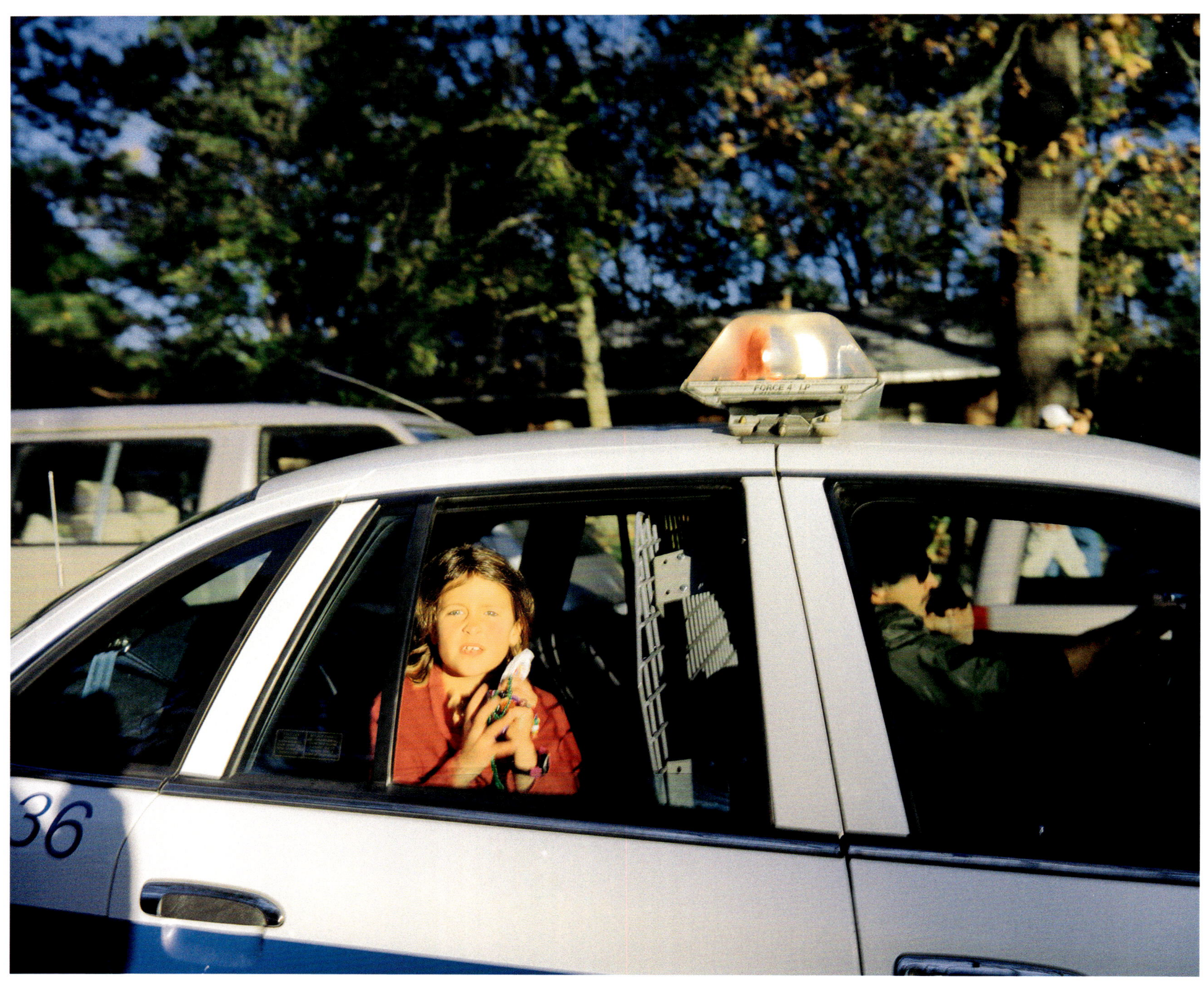
FORCE 4 LP
36

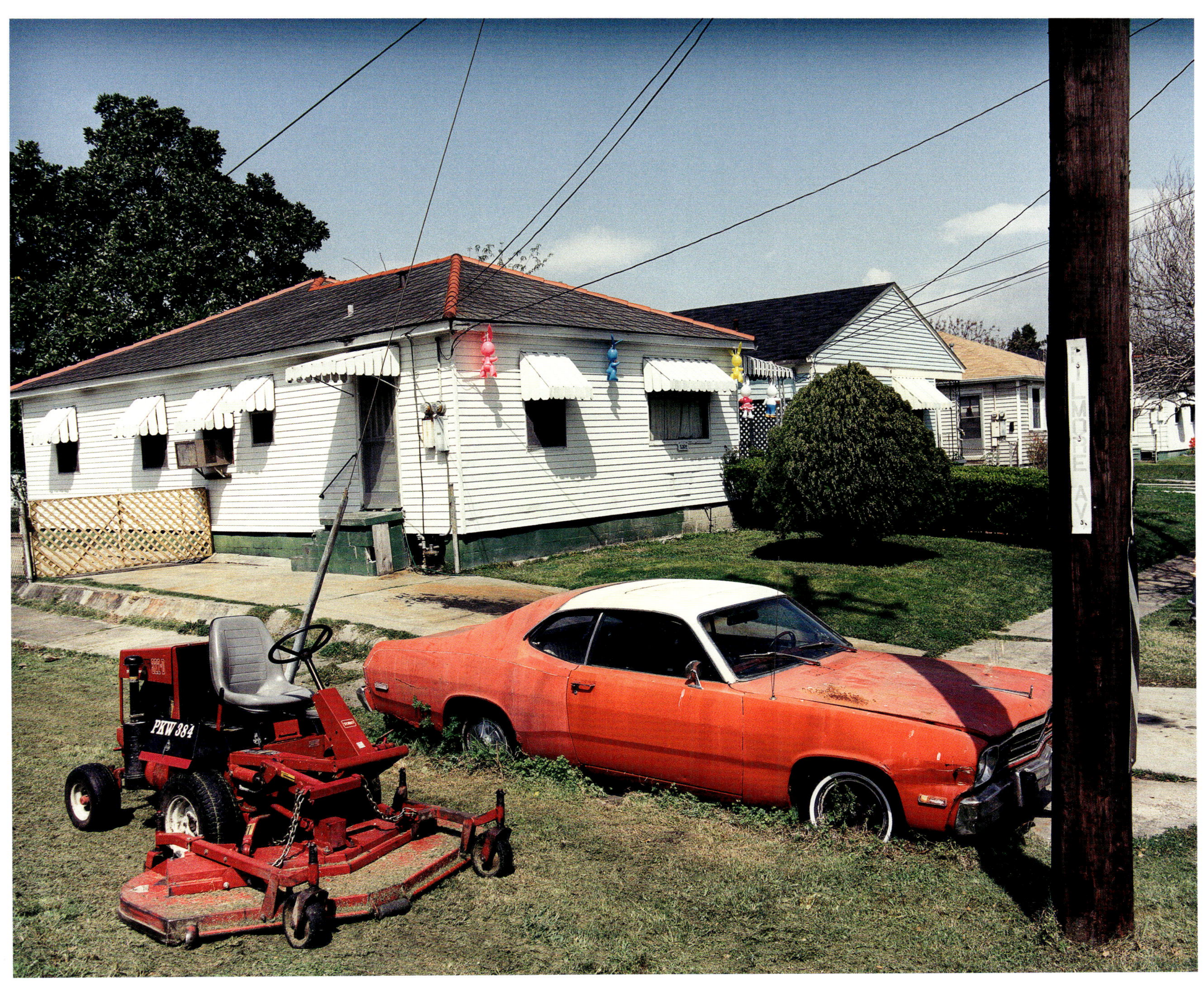
PKW 384
FILMORE AV

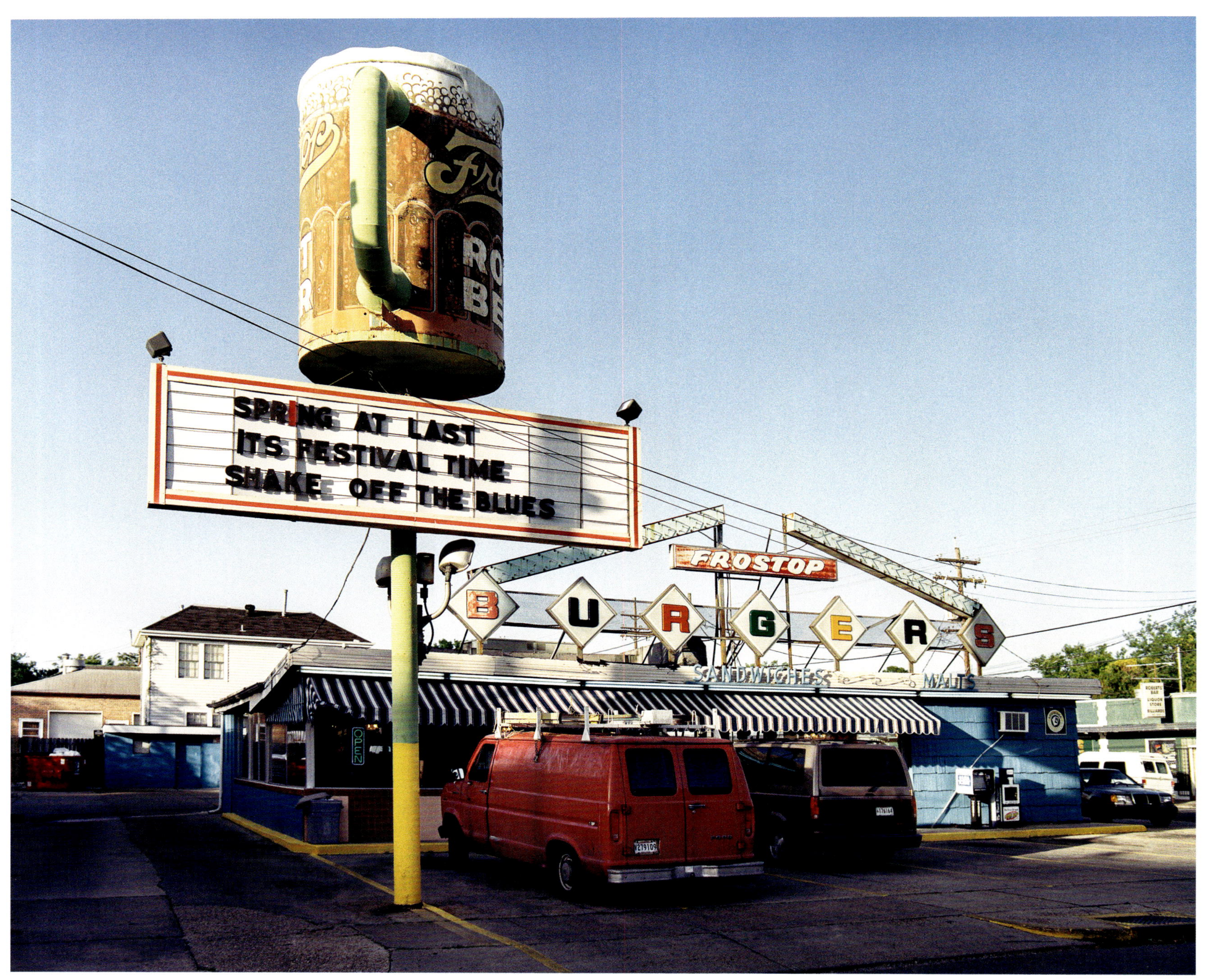
SPRING AT LAST
ITS FESTIVAL TIME
SHAKE OFF THE BLUES
FROSTOP
BURGERS
SANDWICHES
MALTS
OPEN

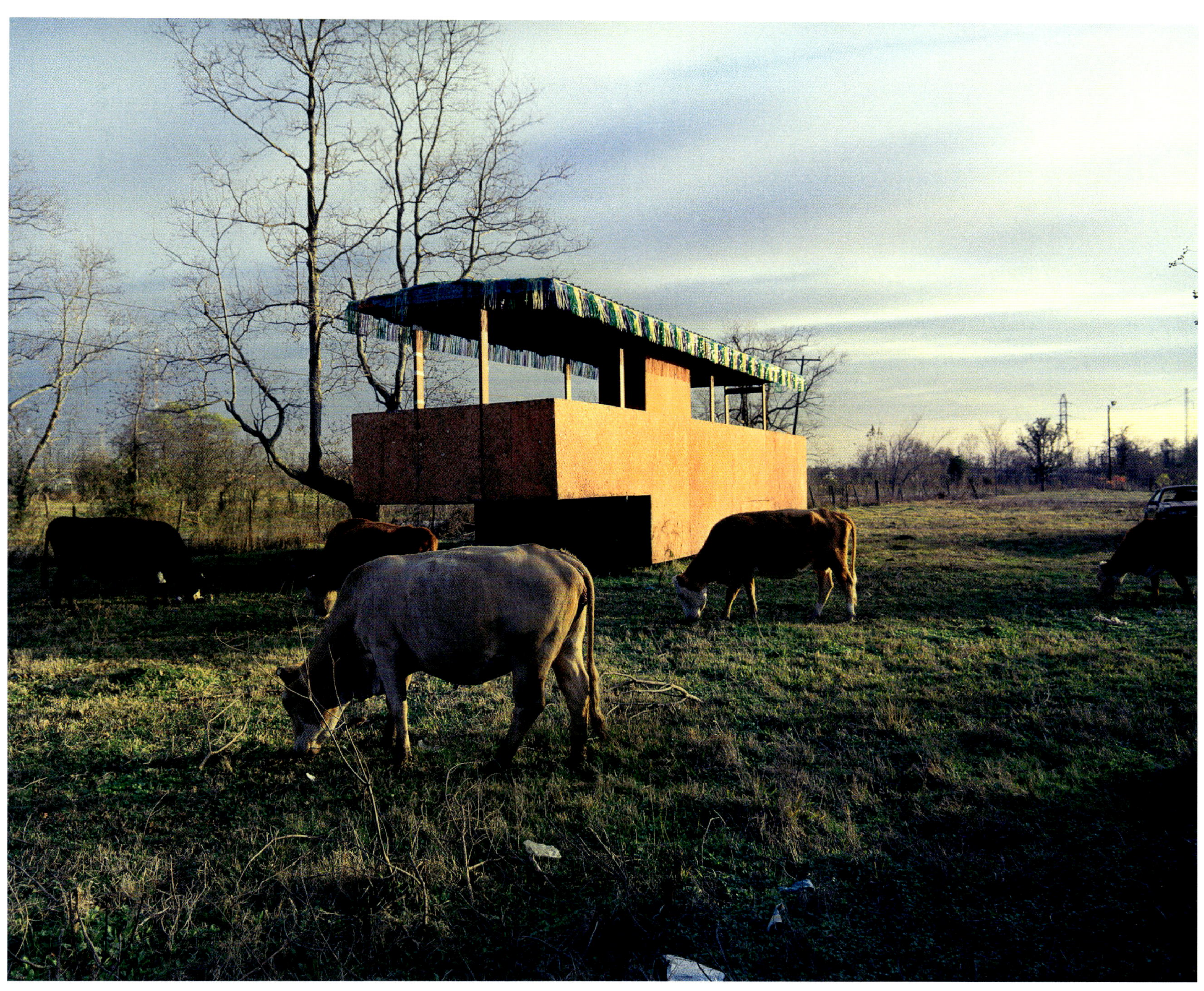

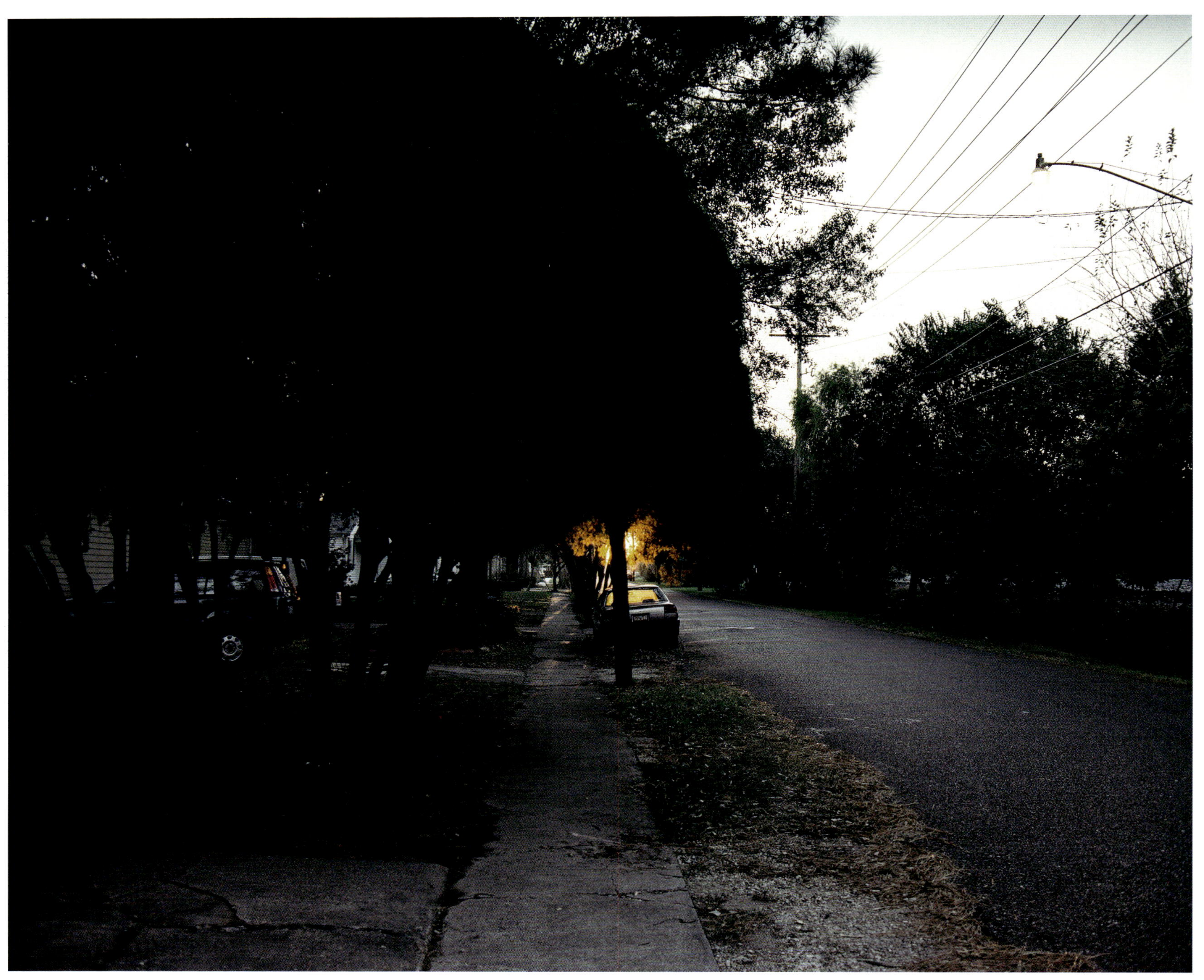

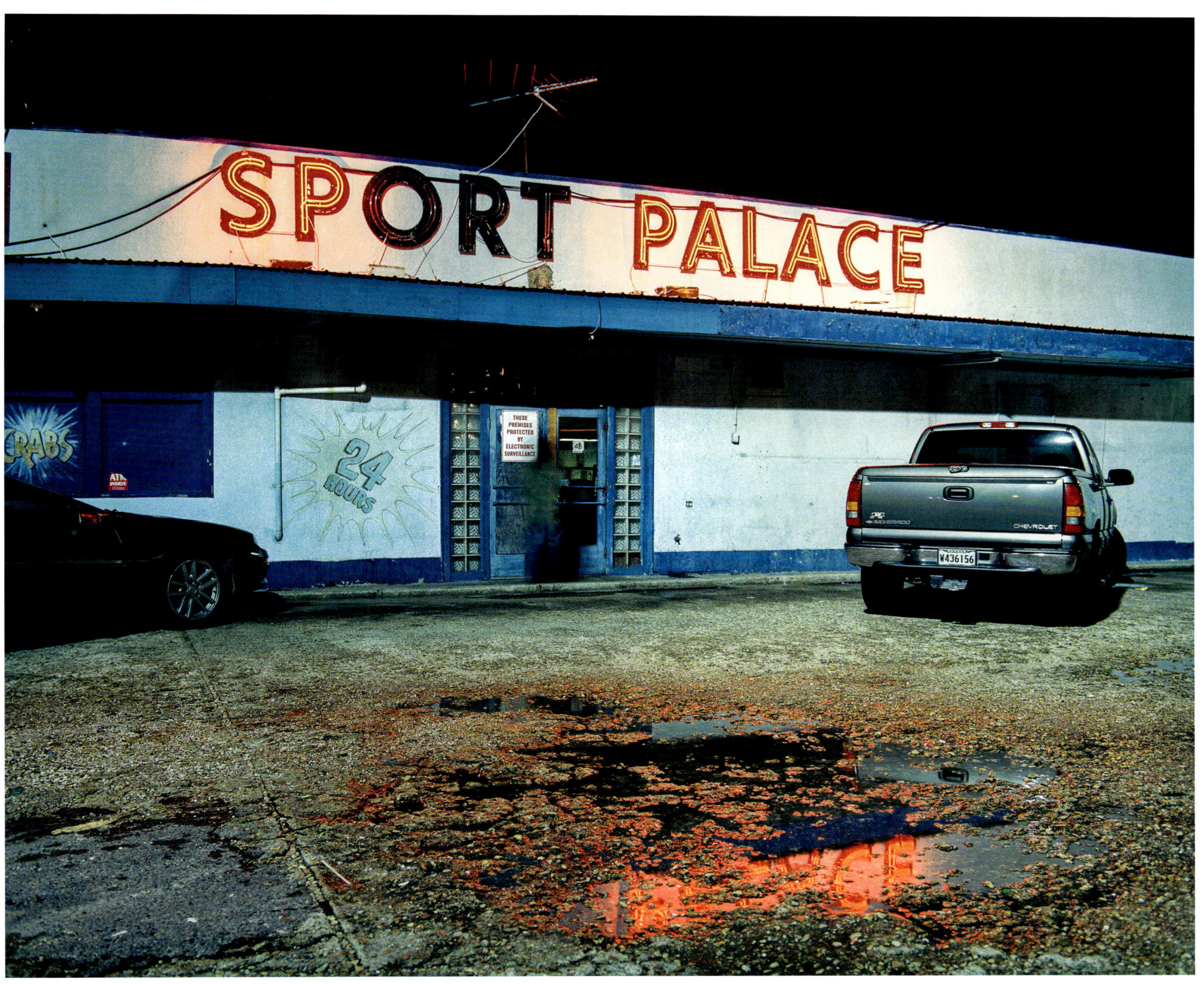
SPORT PALACE
CRABS
24 HOURS
THESE PREMISES PROTECTED BY ELECTRONIC SURVEILLANCE
CHEVROLET
W436156

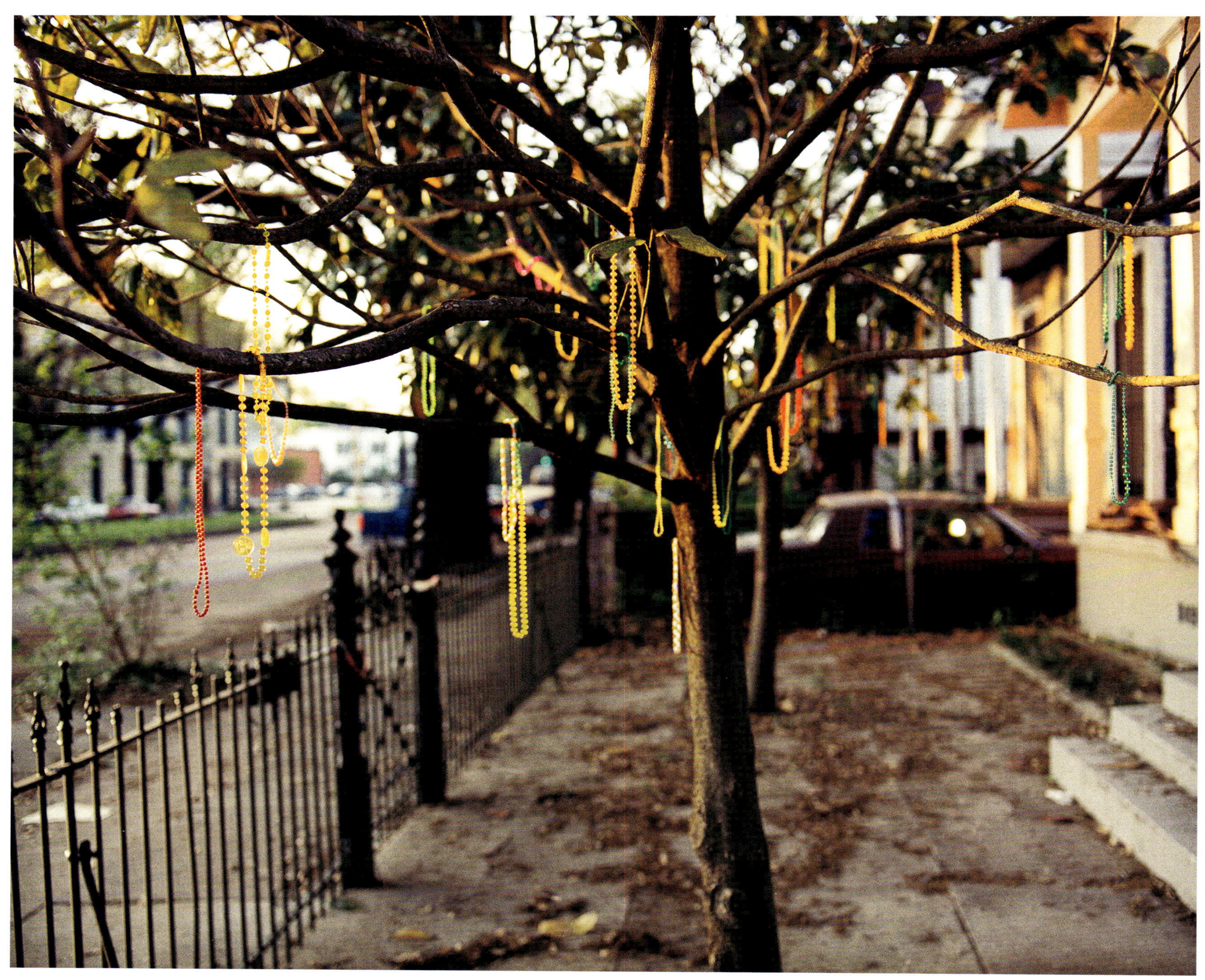

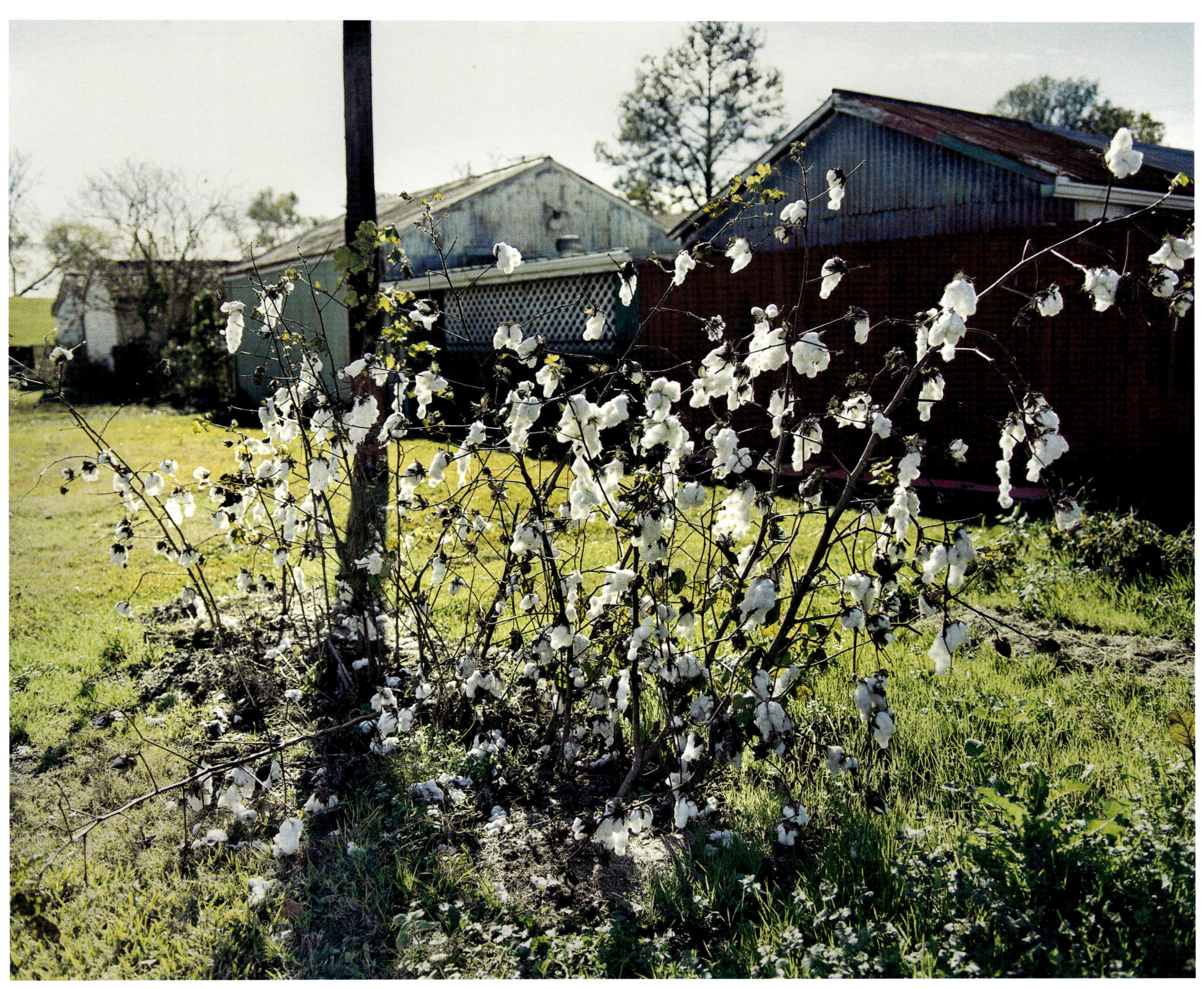

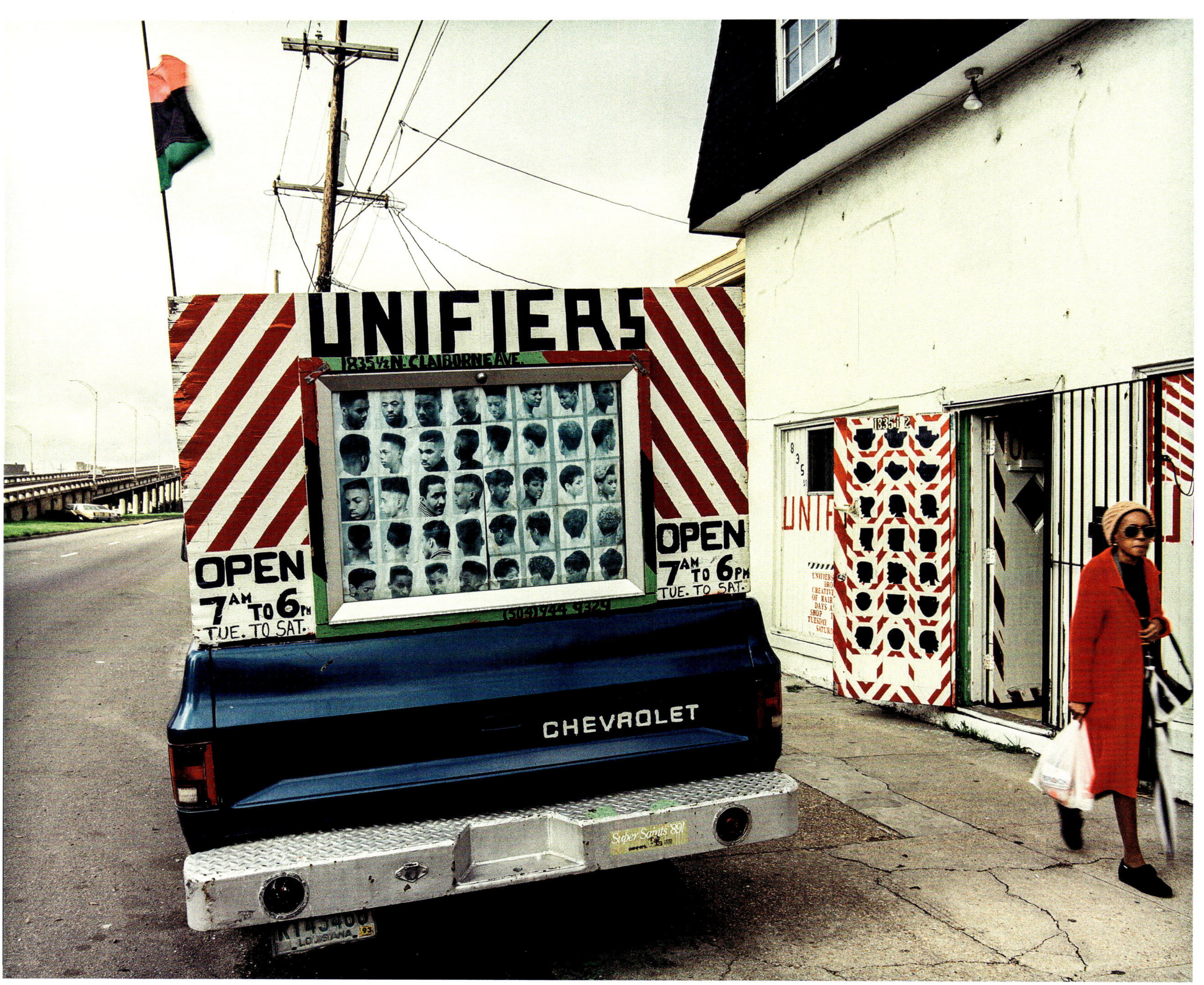
UNIFIERS
OPEN
7AM TO 6PM
TUE. TO SAT.
OPEN
7AM TO 6PM
TUE. TO SAT.
CHEVROLET

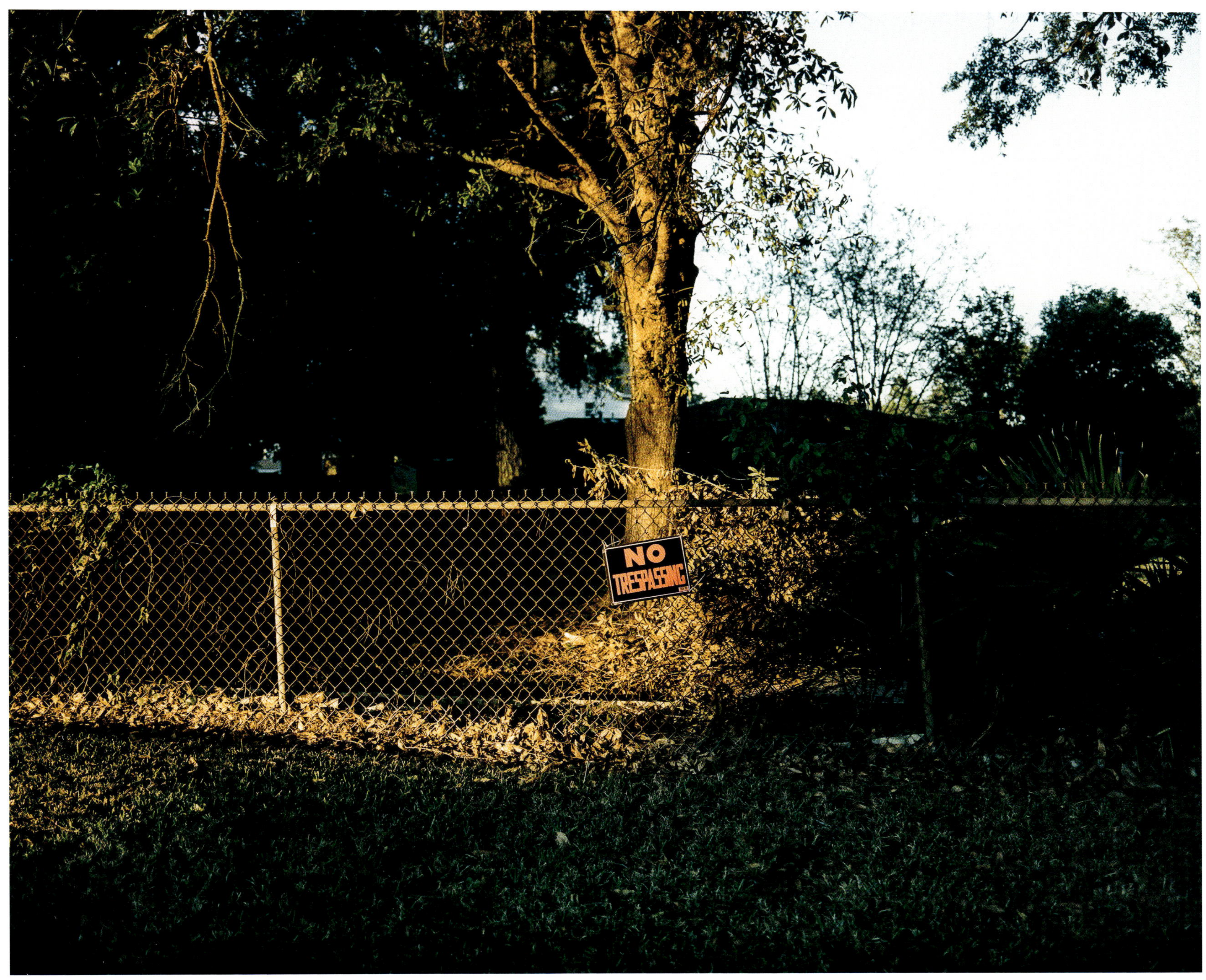
NO
TRESPASSING

NEUTRAL GROUND

NEW ORLEANS 1990–2005

I was born and raised in New Orleans. However, I never fully appreciated how unique a place it was until I went off to college. It then occurred to me that New Orleans was completely singular in its culture, food, architecture, music, art, and colloquialisms. Even the air is unique, soaked in humidity, which affects the light.

As a seven-year-old, in 1965, Hurricane Betsy formed around the date of my birthday, September 8th. Betsy was to be my first experience with a terrifying hurricane but not my last. It left a mark on me. I wondered and worried, how can we live below sea level? Betsy broke levees and flooded low areas of the city. The storm caused a billion dollars in damage.

My last hurricane was some fifty years later, when Katrina struck, again flooding the city. It would be my last experience of the levees breaking. I moved northwest to Baton Rouge, further inland and on higher ground.

The photographs that comprise this book, made between the time of these events and revelations, helped shape how I saw my beloved city.

All images were made in and around New Orleans, between 1990 and 2005.

—WILLIAM GREINER

ACKNOWLEDGMENTS

I would like to express my sincere gratitude to the University of New Orleans Press: editor-in-chief Abram Himelstein, managing editor G.K. Darby, and the entire staff for their enthusiasm and desire to publish this book.

The production would not have been possible without the expert negative scanning and file color-correcting of Mark Berndt. Thank you to Bonnie Campbell for her guidance and technical expertise in layout, design, and everything in between.

The editing and sequencing were done by my dear friends and fellow photographers Alex Harris and Margaret Sartor.

The succinct foreword, written by one of my oldest and dearest friends, John Ramsey Miller, is perfect.

And thank you to a small group of massively talented photographers: Richard Misrach, Stephen Shore, and Birney Imes for letting me bounce book ideas off your keen minds and eyes.

Thank you to the following collectors, patrons, and friends who provided substantial financial support: Wendy Rodrigue and Douglas Magnus, Roger Ogden, Denise Browning and Steve Sumell, Debbie Matoy McNutt, John and Joanna Theriot, Donny Boudreaux, John Ramsey Miller, James and Shannon Quinn, Oliver Fuselier, Randy Haynie, E. Alexandra Stafford, Alexa Georges, Philip Dunham, Margery Gossett, Jason and Kristen Savage, Harry Burglass Jr., Clyde Watkins, and Michael and Rochelle Beychok.

And to my partner in crime and everything else, Jennifer Dyess: Thank you for all your love and support.